# TURKS & CAICOS ISLANDS

Portions of this book appear in *Fodor's Caribbean 2014*.

# 14
## TOP EXPERIENCES

The Turks and Caicos offer terrific experiences that should be on every traveler's list. Here are Fodor's top picks for a memorable trip.

## 1 Grace Bay

One of the world's best beaches, Grace Bay has 12 miles of powdery white sand that frame a calm stretch of turquoise sea. Despite its popularity, you're sure to find some solitude. *(Ch. 2)*

## 2 Coco Bistro

This elegant Providenciales restaurant is popular with vacationers and locals alike for its French- and West Indies–inspired cuisine. *(Ch. 2)*

## 3 Stand-up Paddleboarding

The latest rage on Providenciales is the perfect way to explore the island's lush mangroves. You can also rent a board on Grace Bay. *(Ch. 2)*

### 4 Grand Turk

The atmospheric capital of the Turks and Caicos brims with old Caribbean charm and has beautiful beaches protected by magnificent reefs. *(Ch. 4)*

### 5 Quinton Dean

Celebrated local musician Quinton Dean performs at different venues around Providenciales—when he's not off touring with Prince. Catch a performance if you can. *(Ch. 2)*

### 6 Scuba Diving

Long before luxury resorts attracted beach-goers, divers came to the Turks and Caicos for superb reefs along the Columbus Passage. *(Ch. 4)*

# 7 Sunsets

Gorgeous sunsets can be experienced all over, but the poolside view from Amanyara, a Fodor's Choice resort on Providenciales' far west end, is especially spectacular. *(Ch. 2)*

# 8 Family Fun

Shallow waters, fine sand, and loads of kid-friendly activities make Providenciales one of the Caribbean's best family destinations. *(Ch. 2)*

# 9 Local Color

To see real island culture, go where the locals go: Bugaloo's in Five Cays. Here, you can feast on conch with your feet in the sand and hear live music on Sundays. *(Ch. 2)*

# 10 Half Moon Bay

Accessible only by boat, this natural sandbar rivals Grace Bay for beauty. Go with Caicos Dream Tours for a truly memorable experience. *(Ch. 2)*

# 11 Stingray Encounter

Wade into the shallow waters around Gibbs Cay, a small uninhabited islet off Grand Turk, to swim with stingrays in a natural environment. *(Ch. 4)*

## 12 Whale-watching

From January through April, humpback whales pass so close to Salt Cay that you can see them from the beach. On some days, you can even snorkel with them. *(Ch. 5)*

## 13 Spas

The spas in the Turks and Caicos are some of the Caribbean's finest. Many feature invigorating local conch scrubs and relaxing open-air massages. *(Ch. 2)*

## 14 Seven Stars

Gorgeous inside and out, Seven Stars is the best luxury resort on Providenciales. Even if you don't stay here, be sure to splurge on sundowner drinks on The Deck. *(Ch. 2)*

# CONTENTS

About this Guide . . . . . . . 10

**1 EXPERIENCE THE TURKS AND CAICOS. . . . . . . . . . 11**

Welcome to the
Turks and Caicos . . . . . . . 12

What's Where . . . . . . . . . 14

Turks and Caicos Planner. . . . 16

If You Like . . . . . . . . . . . 18

When to Go . . . . . . . . . . 21

Geography, Flora, and Fauna. . 22

What's New . . . . . . . . . . 23

Kids and Families . . . . . . . 24

**2 PROVIDENCIALES . . . . . 25**

Planning . . . . . . . . . . . . 27

Exploring Providenciales . . . . 31

Beaches . . . . . . . . . . . . 37

Where to Eat. . . . . . . . . . 40

Where to Stay . . . . . . . . . 59

Sports and the Outdoors . . . . 71

Shopping. . . . . . . . . . . . 80

Nightlife . . . . . . . . . . . . 87

An Excursion to West Caicos. . 89

**3 THE CAICOS AND
THE CAYS . . . . . . . . . . . 91**

Planning . . . . . . . . . . . . 92

Little Water Cay . . . . . . . . 94

Pine Cay . . . . . . . . . . . . 95

Fort George Cay. . . . . . . . 96

Dellis Cay . . . . . . . . . . . 97

Parrot Cay . . . . . . . . . . . 97

North Caicos. . . . . . . . . . 99

Middle Caicos . . . . . . . . .104

South Caicos. . . . . . . . . .107

**4 GRAND TURK . . . . . . . 113**

Planning . . . . . . . . . . . .115

Exploring Grand Turk . . . . .117

Beaches . . . . . . . . . . . .119

Where to Eat . . . . . . . . .120

Where to Stay. . . . . . . . .125

Sports and the Outdoors. . . .126

Shopping. . . . . . . . . . . .129

Nightlife . . . . . . . . . . . .130

**5 SALT CAY . . . . . . . . . 131**

Planning . . . . . . . . . . . .132

Exploring Salt Cay. . . . . . .136

Beaches . . . . . . . . . . . .136

Where to Eat . . . . . . . . .137

Where to Stay. . . . . . . . .139

Sports and the Outdoors. . . .141

Shopping. . . . . . . . . . . .142

**TRAVEL SMART TURKS &
CAICOS . . . . . . . . . . . . 143**

**INDEX . . . . . . . . . . . . 161**

**ABOUT OUR WRITER . . . 168**

**MAPS**

Providenciales. . . . . . . 28–29

Grace Bay and
The Bight Dining . . . . . . . 43

Grace Bay and
The Bight Lodging . . . . . . 63

The Caicos & the Cays . . . . . 93

Grand Turk. . . . . . . . . . .116

Cockburn Town . . . . . . . .121

Salt Cay . . . . . . . . . . . .133

# ABOUT THIS GUIDE

### Fodor's Recommendations

Everything in this guide is worth doing—we don't cover what isn't—but exceptional sights, hotels, and restaurants are recognized with additional accolades. Fodor'sChoice★ indicates our top recommendations. Care to nominate a new place? Visit Fodors. com/contact-us.

### Trip Costs

We list prices wherever possible to help you budget well. Hotel and restaurant price categories from **$** to **$$$$** are noted alongside each recommendation. For hotels, we include the lowest cost of a standard double room in high season. For restaurants, we cite the average price of a main course at dinner or, if dinner isn't served, at lunch. For attractions, we always list adult admission fees; discounts are usually available for children, students, and senior citizens.

### Hotels

Our local writers vet every hotel to recommend the best overnights in each price category, from budget to expensive. Unless otherwise specified, you can expect private bath, phone, and TV in your room. For expanded hotel reviews, facilities, and deals visit Fodors.com.

### Restaurants

Unless we state otherwise, restaurants are open for lunch and dinner daily. We mention dress code only when there's a specific requirement and reservations only when they're essential or not accepted. To make restaurant reservations, visit Fodors.com.

### Credit Cards

The hotels and restaurants in this guide typically accept credit cards. If not, we'll say so.

---

**Top Picks**

★ Fodor'sChoice

**Listings**

✉ Address
✉ Branch address
🖅 Mailing address
☎ Telephone
🖶 Fax
⊕ Website
✉ E-mail

🎫 Admission fee
☉ Open/closed times
Ⓜ Subway
✛ Directions or Map coordinates

**Hotels & Restaurants**

🏨 Hotel
🛏 Number of rooms
🍽 Meal plans

✕ Restaurant
🍴 Reservations
👗 Dress code
🚫 No credit cards
$ Price

**Other**

⇨ See also
☞ Take note
🏌 Golf facilities

# 1

# EXPERIENCE THE TURKS AND CAICOS

Visit Fodors.com for advice, updates, and bookings

# WELCOME TO THE TURKS AND CAICOS

The turquoise-color water in the Turks and Caicos is almost electric. Don't be surprised if you wake up on your last morning and realize you never strayed far from the beach or those mesmerizing views. Although ivory-white, soft, sandy beaches and breathtaking turquoise waters are shared among all the islands, the landscapes are a series of contrasts, from the dry, arid bush and scrub on the flat, coral islands of Grand Turk, Salt Cay, South Caicos, and Providenciales to the greener, foliage-rich undulating landscapes of Middle Caicos, North Caicos, Parrot Cay, and Pine Cay.

## Discovery

A much-disputed legend tells us that Columbus first discovered these islands on his first voyage to the New World in 1492. Although known and explored for longer than most other island groups in the southern Atlantic and Caribbean, the Turks and Caicos islands (pronounced *kay*-kos) still remain part of the less-discovered Caribbean. More than 40 islands—only eight of which are inhabited—make up this self-governing British overseas territory that lies just 575 miles (862 km) southeast of Miami on the third-largest coral reef system in the world.

## Changing Hands

The Turks and Caicos have been claimed by France and Spain, and by Bermuda in the late 1600s. Bermuda wanted the islands for their salt—at the time it was as highly sought after as gold—and for land on which to grow cotton. Sea Island cotton, believed to be the highest quality, was produced on the Loyalist plantations in the Caicos Islands from the 1700s. For a time, Salt Cay provided much of the salt that supplied the United States and Canada.

## Reefs and Wrecks

It's estimated that some 1,000 shipwrecks surround the islands. Some island residents can trace their ancestry back to the wreck of the Spanish slave ship *Trouvadore,* which ran aground off East Caicos in 1841; the surviving slaves helped populate these islands. But the most famous wreck is probably of the Spanish galleon *Nuestra Senora de la Concepcion,* which sank after hitting a shallow reef in 1641 in the Silver Shoals, between the Turks and Caicos and what is now the Dominican Republic. By 1687, William Phips had recovered a small portion of the treasure, but the larger part was not discovered until 1978, by Burt Webber. The wreck contained treasure worth millions, as well as priceless artifacts, including porcelain from the late Ming period.

## Tumultuous Times

The 1700s were a tumultuous time for the Turks and Caicos and the era when piracy first began to be a force. In 1718, two female pirates, Anne Bonny and Mary Read, captured a Spanish treasure ship and its cargo, then settled on Pirate Cay, which is now known as Parrot Cay. In 1720, a pirate named Francoise L'Olonnois lived in French Cay, which he used as a base to raid passing ships. On Providenciales, at Splitting Rock (sometimes called Osprey Rock), there are carvings on the rocks that are reputedly maps to buried treasures. In 1783, the French seized Grand Turk again, but the islands were restored to Britain by the Treaty of Versailles.

## The People

In all, only 31,500 people live in the Turks and Caicos islands; more than half are "Belongers," the term for the native population, mainly descended from African and Bermudian slaves who settled here beginning in the 1600s. The majority of residents work in tourism, fishing, and offshore finance, as the country is a haven for the overtaxed. Indeed, for residents and visitors, life in "TCI" is anything but taxing. Although most visitors come to do nothing—a specialty in the islands—this does not mean there's nothing to do.

## The Rise of Providenciales

The political and historical capital island of the country is Grand Turk, but most of the tourism development is on Providenciales (usually shortened to Provo), thanks to the 12-mile (18-km) stretch of ivory sand that is Grace Bay. Once home to a population of around 500 people plus a few donkey carts, Provo has become a hub of activity since the 1990s, as resorts, spas, and restaurants have been built and as the population has grown to some 15,000. It's the temporary home for the vast majority of visitors who come to the Turks and Caicos islands.

## Remnants of History

Marks of the country's colonial past can be found in the wood-and-stone Bermudian-style clapboard houses—often wrapped in deep-red bougainvillea—that line the streets on the quiet islands of Grand Turk, Salt Cay, and South Caicos. Donkeys roam free in and around the islands' many salt ponds, which are a legacy from a time when residents worked hard as both slaves and then paid laborers to rake salt (then known as "white gold") bound for the United States and Canada. Much of this history is recounted in the national museum on Grand Turk.

# WHAT'S WHERE

**1** **Providenciales.** Provo has the lion's share of accommodations in the Turks and Caicos and gets the lion's share of visitors. Come if you are seeking miles of soft sand, luxurious accommodations, crystal-clear water, and fine dining in gorgeous settings. Don't come for nightlife or shopping—there are few hot spots and even fewer fancy boutiques.

**2** **The Caicos and the Cays.** The private-island resorts are ultraluxurious, but several of the cays are uninhabited. South Caicos is all about diving; on North and Middle Caicos, you'll feel like you're stepping back in time to a simpler Caribbean. If you can afford it, try the pampering at Parrot Cay or the Meridien Club.

**3** **Grand Turk.** The historic capital of the Turks and Caicos gets many more visitors by cruise ship than as overnight guests. Come here if you like to dive or just relax, and if you're on a budget, you'll find that prices are more reasonable than those on Provo.

**4** **Salt Cay.** Step off the ferry or plane here and you may feel as if you landed in 1950. Come to relax on the prettiest beach in all the Turks and Caicos, and to meet people who might become lifelong friends. In season, you may want to watch whales. Don't come expecting more than rustic accommodations and patchy service.

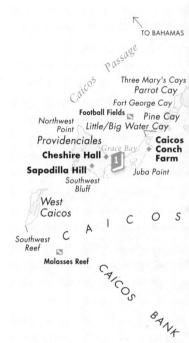

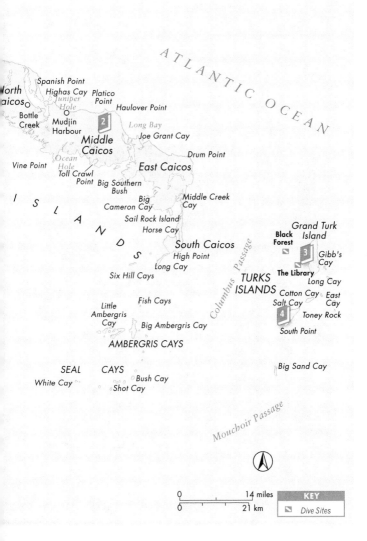

ATLANTIC OCEAN

North Caicos

Spanish Point
Highas Cay
Juniper Hole
Platico Point
Haulover Point
Bottle Creek
Mudjin Harbour
Middle Caicos
Long Bay
Joe Grant Cay
Drum Point
Vine Point
Ocean Hole
Toll Crawl Point
East Caicos
Big Southern Bush
Big Cameron Cay
Middle Creek Cay
Sail Rock Island
Horse Cay
I S L A N D S
South Caicos
High Point
Long Cay
Six Hill Cays
Little Ambergris Cay
Fish Cays
Big Ambergris Cay
AMBERGRIS CAYS

Grand Turk Island
Black Forest
Gibb's Cay
The Library
Long Cay
Cotton Cay
Salt Cay
East Cay
Toney Rock
South Point

Columbus Passage

TURKS ISLANDS

SEAL CAYS
White Cay
Bush Cay
Shot Cay

Big Sand Cay

Mouchoir Passage

0        14 miles
0        21 km

KEY
◳ Dive Sites

# TURKS AND CAICOS PLANNER

## Essentials

**Currency:** The official currency on the islands is the U.S. dollar, so there is never a need to change money.

**Electricity:** Current is suitable for all U.S. appliances, and electrical plugs are just like those you have at home.

**Passport Requirements:** A valid passport is required, and everyone must have an ongoing or return ticket.

**Phones:** The country code for the Turks and Caicos is 649, though calls go through just as if you were another U.S. number (though they are charged as international calls). Calls from the islands are expensive, and many hotels add a steep surcharge. U.S. GSM cell phones work throughout the islands, but many car rental companies provide pay-as-you-go loaner phones for free.

## Getting Here and Around

**Air Travel:** Several major airlines fly nonstop to Providenciales from the United States, including American (DFW and MIA), United (EWR), Delta (ATL), JetBlue (BOS, JFK), and US Airways (BOS, CLT, PHL). You can also fly from a few other spots in the Caribbean on Air Turks & Caicos or from the Bahamas on Bahamas Air.

**Car Rentals:** You can get by on Provo without a car, especially if you are staying in the hub of Grace Bay. Rentals are relatively inexpensive on Provo (much more elsewhere), but you have to pay for a temporary driving permit. Gas is also expensive and must often be paid for in cash (except at a couple of Texaco stations on Provo). And don't forget that driving is on the left.

**Island Hopping:** You can make air connections to three other islands from Providenciales (Grand Turk, South Caicos, and Salt Cay). There's also daily ferry service between Provo and North Caicos and from Grand Turk to Salt Cay and from Middle Caicos to South Caicos. A causeway connects North Caicos to Middle Caicos. Other islands can be reached by charter flight or boat.

**Taxis:** You can find taxis at the airports in Provo and Grand Turk, but they can be expensive. Fares are set by the government and include two bags per person. On both Grand Turk and South Caicos you need to arrange your airport pickup in advance.

## Accommodations

Most accommodations on Providenciales are condo-style, but not all resorts are family-friendly. You'll find several upscale properties on the family (outer) islands, including the famous Parrot Cay, but the majority of places there are small inns, not full-fledged resorts. What you give up in luxury, however, you gain back tenfold in island charm.

Villas and condos are plentiful, particularly on Provo, and usually represent a good value for families, who will appreciate the extra space to spread out, the full kitchens (usually fully equipped), and the laundry facilities. With demand high, especially in the busy season, it makes sense to plan as far ahead as possible.

## Saving Money

Although the Turks and Caicos are fairly expensive vacation destinations, there are ways to save. The local website ⊕ *TurksandCaicosReservations.tc* works directly with the resorts to offer additional discounts and deals. Traveling during non-peak season, when many resorts offer free nights and extra perks, is another way to save. If you don't mind being a block or two from the beach, you can even save more. And you can cook some meals yourself. Airlines will allow you to bring a cooler of food as long as perishables are frozen and vacuum sealed; this strategy could save you some money, especially on meat.

## Visitor Information

You can get information about the islands from the Turks & Caicos Islands Tourist Board (⊕ *www. turksandcaicostourism. com*). Tourist offices on Providenciales and Grand Turk are open daily from 9 to 5. Visitors should also check out ⊕ *www. wherewhenhow.com*, a terrific source with links to every place to stay, all the restaurants, excursions, and transportation on Providenciales (and to a lesser degree the other islands).

## Weddings

The residency requirement is 48 hours, after which you can apply for a marriage license at the registrar in Grand Turk. Using a local wedding planner who can help make all the arrangements as well as file all the appropriate legal paperwork can be useful. One experienced company is Nila Destinations Wedding Planning (⊕ *www. nilavacations.com*).

# IF YOU LIKE

### The best beaches in the world

The main reason most people come to Turks and Caicos is for the beautiful beaches, which make everyone's top-10 list. At least one of these beaches will make yours, too. These flat, dry islands with fine coral sand are surrounded by crystal-clear waters that appear almost neon blue. The water is so bright in some places that it glows. And when you think the beach can't be better or prettier than the last one you were on, it is. If you're lucky, sometimes you might have a beautiful strand all to yourself.

And even amidst the general beauty, some places stand out. People come to Turks and Caicos to see Grace Bay: 12 miles (18 km) of uninterrupted neon blue, with no rocks or seaweed, and powder-fine sand that won't burn your feet even in the heat of the day. If you can break away from Grace Bay, you'll be rewarded with many other exquisite strands right on Provo. Malcolm's Beach has even bluer water (you must brave the adventurous road that leads to it), and Pelican Beach has tons of bright-white conch shells you can bring back home. On any of the cays you may have the beaches to yourself. Half Moon Bay and Fort George are a photographer's delight, with curves in the sand, shells, and palms. Pine Cay might have one of the best strands: no rocks, just a long, secluded, gorgeous beach. Mudjin Harbour on Middle Caicos is the most scenic, surrounded by towering cliffs and isolated coves; around one T-shape coral cliff, waves crash on one side while the other is as calm as glass; at high tide the water meets in the middle. The most beautiful beach of all is North Beach on Salt Cay; with its perfect-color water and clean soft sand, you'll never want to leave.

### The best deep-sea fishing

A Turks and Caicos vacation is all about being on the water. From the bright turquoise waters to the beautiful mangroves to the flats of the Caicos Bank, you can have your pick of watery environments. And one of the best ways to experience the best of Turks and Caicos is to take one of the many fishing excursions. Deep-sea, bone-, or bottom fishing are your choices, and a boat will allow you to see otherwise unreachable parts of the islands.

Bonefishing is exciting. Bonefish live in the shallow flats of the smaller cays and Middle Caicos. You'll get an up-close look at mangroves and the wildlife. The fishing itself is challenging and exciting. Your casting technique and endurance will be tested by the bonefish—they're relentless fighters. The key to a great trip is a great guide, and Arthur Dean at Silver Deep is one of the best. His extensive knowledge of the Turks and Caicos flats and his respect for the wildlife and the environment will leave you feeling that your money was well spent.

## Excellent diving

With the third-largest barrier reef in the world, dramatic walls that drop from 20 feet to more than 6,000 feet, and mostly sunny days shining on crystal-clear, calm waters, the Turks and Caicos are a diver's dream destination. The steep sea walls close to the shore usually prevent waves from churning the water, and sea creatures thrive on these reefs. The visibility is consistently some of the best in the world, averaging 100 to 200 feet on most days. The Turks and Caicos were put on the map as a dive destination, and these waters are still one of the great places in the world to dive.

Each island in the archipelago boasts excellent dive spots. Providenciales has terrific reefs at Northwest Point. West Caicos has Spanish galleon shipwrecks and sudden drop-offs that are so deep they appear to be purple from the surface. Grand Turk has dramatic walls close to shore, so you can spend more time div-ing and less time reaching the sites. Salt Cay not only has sections of pristine reef that you will have virtually all to yourself, but the immediate area has excellent wreck diving and offers one of the best opportunities in the world to swim with whales in season. The best of the best is probably South Caicos, which claims to have the best visibility in the world, not to mention miles of untouched reefs waiting to be discovered. Expect to see sharks, dolphins, colorful reef fish, stingrays, and lobsters wherever you dive.

## Great snorkeling

If you're not a certified diver, then the next-best thing (and perhaps the very best thing for most) is to take a half- or full-day snorkeling excursion to one of the many uninhabited cays and secluded coves. There are many companies to choose from, and all the trips can give you a great experience. Some trips are on catamarans, some on powerboats. Some companies allow you to dive for conch, some to snorkel for sand dollars. Some boats stop at Iguana Island to see the iguanas, some stop to let you snorkel on the reef, some stop to find the cannons in the water. But all stop on one of the cays so you can experience a quiet, secluded beach.

If you want a more private experience, then have a boat drop you off on one of many secluded beaches for the day, leaving you with a cooler full of food and drink, along with beach chairs, umbrellas, and snorkel gear. Then you can snorkel directly from the beach. You'll often be alone. Half Moon Bay is one of the most pristine spots for this kind of beach day, with sugar-white sand that lends itself to excellent swimming, brilliant snorkeling, and opportunities to walk and explore on land. Limestone cliffs frame the cove, and iguanas are the only residents. If you budget for only one trip, then go here.

## A new island every day

With eight inhabited islands, you can visit a different island every day of your weeklong stay in the Turks and Caicos. From Provo's Walkin Marina, you can take the daily ferry over to North Caicos, rent a car, and go on a quest to find secluded beaches. If you rent a car in North Caicos, you can drive over the causeway to Middle Caicos to visit limestone caves or hike the trails next to its glorious coves. During whale-watching season (mid-January to mid-April), you can hop over to Salt Cay, where whales get so close you can reach out and touch them. One of the best day trips is to Grand Turk,

with its laid-back charm and old Caribbean architecture.

Air Turks and Caicos offers early-morning flights to Grand Turk that return the same day. It's only a 30-minute flight to the tiny island, and touring everything Grand Turk has to offer will leave plenty of time for the beach. You can stroll down Front Street to see its original clapboard buildings, and say hi to the wild horses and roosters that share the walk with you. You can stop at the beautiful Anglican church with its bright white walls and even brighter red gate and walk past the bright-pink government house. Don't forget to stop at the excellent museum. There's a lighthouse at the tip of the island. You can swim with peaceful stingrays on an excursion to Gibbs Cay. If there's a cruise ship at the port you can shop at the Ron Jon surf shop, Piranha Joe's, and the largest Margaritaville in the world. Stop at the Sand Bar on the way back to the airport for a drink on the deck over the water and get to know the locals, then return to Provo in time for a delicious dinner.

# WHEN TO GO

Peak season in the Turks and Caicos runs from December 15 to April 15—just as in the Caribbean—when prices average 20% to 50% higher than in the summer months. This is also when the beaches are the most crowded. January through March can bring on "Christmas Winds" and the resulting swells, even on Grace Bay. Both water and air temperatures in the Turks and Caicos are cooler than those in the Caribbean, especially in the months before March.

## Climate

Temperatures in the Turks and Caicos islands range from 75°F to 85°F year-round, except during the hottest months of August and September. The islands are among the driest in the Caribbean and southern Atlantic region, with an average of 350 days of sunshine, light trade winds, and less humidity than in surrounding islands. Water temperatures range from the high 70s in the winter to the low 80s in the summer; generally, the water here is cooler than in the Caribbean until March. Hurricane season runs from June through November. Hurricanes are rare; two hurricanes in September 2008 were the first storms to strike the islands directly in 50 years.

## Festivals and Events

Every month has an annual event, check ⊕ *enews.tc* for actual dates. During festivities extra transportation is provided when needed (at a cost).

**January:** The Junkanoo New Year's Eve street party with live bands, parades, and fireworks happens in Grace Bay. The Winter Wahoo Fishing Tournament is held at Turtle Cove.

**May:** The South Caicos Regatta is held on South Caicos during the last weekend in May (⊕ *bigsouthregatta.tc*).

**August:** The annual Provo Days Festival (end of July to the beginning of August) features music battle of the bands, beauty contests and vendor booths, Provo.

**October:** The annual Rake n' Scrape festival on North Caicos happens at the end of October, with live bands all day, domino competitions with cash prizes, and face painting and a bouncing castle for kids.

**December:** The Maskanoo Street party and parade is held on Boxing Day (December 26), offering live bands, vendors, food stalls, party favors, and a parade on Grace Bay Road in the middle of the hub in Provo. This is a must-see post-Christmas celebration.

# GEOGRAPHY, FLORA, AND FAUNA

The landscape in the Turks and Caicos is flat—even the hills aren't very high—and dry; although not a true desert, the chain experiences the least amount of rainfall of any island nation in the southern Atlantic and Caribbean. The sand around the shoreline is made up of crushed coral stone, which has a bright white color and makes the sea appear more turquoise than almost anywhere else in the Caribbean.

## Birds

French Cay is a bird-watcher's dream, protected as a national park. Here you can see dozens of white-cheeked pintail, reddish egrets, and osprey. The country's national bird, the osprey, can be seen on all the islands, but osprey nests are easier to see at Three Mary Cays on North Caicos or at Splitting Rock, also known as Osprey Rock, on Provo. Bright pink flamingos can be spotted on some islands, especially at Flamingo Pond at North Caicos, the pond at West Caicos, and at Provo's only golf course.

## Flora

The official national plant is the Turks head cactus, so named because of its shape. The body is round, and it's topped with a red cylinder, which resembles a Turkish fez (hat). The best place to see fields of them is on Ambergris Cay. Silver palms grow naturally in the scrub, adding a tropical flair to beaches such as Half Moon Bay, but the trees are most numerous on West Caicos. North Caicos is considered the "garden" island, as it receives the most rainfall of the islands and is greener as a result. The cays all have small limestone cliffs that have formed from years of ocean waves.

## Other Fauna

Huge blue land crabs come out in the spring after rains. You're more likely to spot one on the sparsely populated islands of North and Middle Caicos, although they can be seen on Provo, too. The queen conchs that thrive in the flats between Provo and Little Water Cay are an important part of the islands' economies. The Turks and Caicos have the largest population of conch in the world, and conch is the most important food on these islands. Conch diving and deep-sea fishing both require fishing permits. The most important indigenous species of the Turks and Caicos is the rock iguana. They're mostly found at Little Water Cay, which is also known as Iguana Island. So beloved are these iguanas that Little Water Cay has been declared a national park. Excursion companies will make a stop to view them.

# WHAT'S NEW

There are several major developments in progress in the Turks and Caicos at this writing. One of the biggest resort expansions on Provo happened in 2013, when Beaches bought the former Veranda resort, changing the name to "Key West Village," to create one of the chain's biggest and best resorts. The water park in the new section is adding a thrilling "Sky Slide" at this writing.

Several major chains, including JW Marriott and Hilton, are in the later planning stages, with resorts aimed to open by 2016. The Marriott has even broken ground on its nine-story, 380-room resort with 16 residential condos.

At this writing, Blue Haven Resort was set to open on the former Nikki Beach site at Leeward Marina in 2013. The resort has a private beach, and the marina can berth yachts up to 220 feet in length. The casual restaurant, Salt, has already opened for business.

The Shore Club will bring life to the secluded Long Bay Beach, a property developed by the popular Hartling Group of Regent Palms and the Sands Resorts. With only 38 suites, it will also have three pools and a spa. Guests will have Long Bay Beach mostly to themselves because there are no other beachfront properties there.

Development is not limited to Providenciales. In West Caicos activity is starting up again at the abandoned Molasses Reef site, once set to become a Ritz-Carlton. This will bring new life to an uninhabited island.

Last Chance Bar and Grill on North Caicos has plans to build a suspended deck over the flats to offer an even more amazing view to diners.

The biggest changes will be in South Caicos. Vacationers hardly venture there because it has so little tourism infrastructure. However, the new East Bay Resort is scheduled to open by 2014; around the same time, Sail Rock Resort will provide private villa rentals for quiet getaways. East Bay Resort, when completed, will be full service with a restaurant and bar, business center, health club and spa, and tour desk. The tour desk can arrange diving and snorkeling, fishing tours, and water sports. When these resorts open, Caribbean Cruisin' will increase ferry service to South Caicos from Provo. Ferry service will allow day trips from Provo for scuba diving. Big Blue based in Provo will also launch day trips including scuba diving trips to South Caicos.

# KIDS AND FAMILIES

The Turks and Caicos offer a number of wonderful family activities, and not all of them are on Provo. While most of the family-friendly activities are on Providenciales, the rest of the islands—especially Grand Turk—provide plenty of other options for family fun.

## Accommodations

Although Provo and the rest of the Turks and Caicos have several resorts, most of the accommodations are in private rental villas or condo-style apartments. These are ideal for families because they offer more space as well as cooking and often laundry facilities.

## In Provo

Other than the beach, Providenciales has the greatest number of other sights and activities. At the **Caicos Conch Farm,** not only do kids learn about the biggest export from the Turks and Caicos Islands, but they can meet the most famous resident, Sally. **Coral Gardens** is an easy zero-entry reef for off-the-beach snorkeling; it's great for kids because they can start seeing colorful fish in waist-high water. For kids with more swimming skills (or when they get braver) buoys mark the spot where the water starts getting much deeper and where they can see bigger fish as they gain confidence. The Bight's **public playground** has swing sets and slides, along with bathrooms and vending machines. **Little Water Cay** (aka Iguana Island) is a stone's throw away from Leeward, with wooden plank paths to help you search for iguanas, who are not really at all elusive here. And if these aren't enough activities for the kids, they can always ride **banana boats** on Grace Bay.

## Outer Islands

Beyond Provo there's still a lot to attract families. On Middle Caicos, kids can check out the small, hand-carved boats at **Middle Caicos Co-op. Mudjin Harbour** has caves with bats and hiking trails on cliffs ending in a hidden staircase to a cave and "secret" beach.

Grand Turk has a terrific museum, **Turks and Caicos National Museum,** and its collection is filled with things that kids love: pirates, moon landings, and the biggest collection of "messages in a bottle" found anywhere. **Her Majesty's Prison** always seems to fascinate children with a glimpse of how prisons used to be. **Gibb's Cay** is always a favorite of kids, offering them a chance to play and hold gentle stingrays on a secluded "Gilligan's Island."

# PROVIDENCIALES

By
Ramona
Settle

**PASSENGERS TYPICALLY BECOME SILENT** when their plane starts its descent to the Providenciales airport, mesmerized by the shallow, crystal-clear, turquoise waters of Chalk Sound National Park. This island, nicknamed Provo, was once called Blue Hills, after its first settlement. Just south of the airport and downtown area, Blue Hills remains most like a traditional Caicos Island settlement on this, the most developed part of the island chain. Most of the modern resorts, exquisite spas, water-sports operators, shops, business plazas, restaurants, bars, cafés, and the championship golf course are on or close by the 12-mile- (18-km-) long Grace Bay. In spite of the ever-increasing number of taller and grander condominium resorts—many have popped up since the late 1990s—it's still possible to find deserted stretches on this priceless, ivory-white shoreline. For guaranteed seclusion, rent a car and explore the southern shores and western tip of the island, or set sail for a private island getaway on one of the many deserted cays nearby.

Providenciales, which has the highest concentration of resorts as well as the country's biggest airport, is where most tourists are headed when they come to the Turks and Caicos. Regardless of which other island you may be going to, you'll stop here first. Accommodations and dining here are expensive; Provo is an upscale destination. Even souvenirs are costly; you won't find T-shirts for less than $25, for example. But you won't be hassled here as you might be in less expensive destinations. Beach vendors won't approach you—you have to approach them to buy. Provo is a great place to de-stress and unwind.

All this progress and beauty comes at a price: with plenty of new visitors arriving each year, the country's charms are no longer a secret, but don't worry—you'll still enjoy the gorgeous beaches and wonderful dinners. Although you may start to believe that every road leads to a big resort development, there are, happily, plenty of sections of beach where you can escape the din.

**THE ELUSIVE GREEN FLASH. Does it really exist?** You may hear that just as the sun sets on the horizon, on nights where the conditions are perfect, you can see a flash of neon-green light. If you blink, you'll miss it. Your best chance to spot it is on a cloudless day with no haze—and you must have a clear view of the sun as it sinks below the horizon. There is much debate whether this phenomenon exists. Some islanders claim to have seen it; others are skeptical. If you want to catch the elusive green flash, Provo—with little haze and often a clear view of the horizon—is one of the best places to try.

# PLANNING

## GETTING HERE AND AROUND

### AIR TRAVEL

All international flights arrive in Providenciales; from here there are regularly scheduled flights to Grand Turk, Salt Cay, and South Caicos (or to almost any of the islands on a charter). Both Air Turks & Caicos and Caicos Express offer regularly scheduled flights around the islands.

Security lines can be brutal at the airport in Providenciales, which has difficulty handling the large number of departures on busy weekends. The holding area, while covered, is outdoors and not air-conditioned, so many people opt to pay for expedited handling and access to the small VIP lounge at the airport through VIP Flyers Club. The cost is $200 for the first person in a group and $75 for each additional person, and you get priority security screening and check-in, and are then whisked away to the 15-person lounge. You can also get access only to the lounge, though on very busy days there may be no time to relax before your flight. During the high season, this service should be booked as far in advance as possible as there is very limited availability.

**Contacts Air Turks & Caicos** ☎ *649/941–5481* ⊕ *www.airturksandcaicos.com.* **Caicos Express** ☎ *649/243–0237* ⊕ *caicosexpressairways.com.* **VIP Flyers Club** ☎ *646/340–9602 in the U.S., 649/946–4000 in Providenciales, 866/587–6168 toll-free* ⊕ *www.vipflyersclub.com.*

### GROUND TRANSPORTATION

Taxis are available after all arriving international flights. Almost no resorts are permitted to provide shuttle service, so even if you are met at the airport by a representative of your resort you will be put into a regular taxi in most cases (unless you have rented a car).

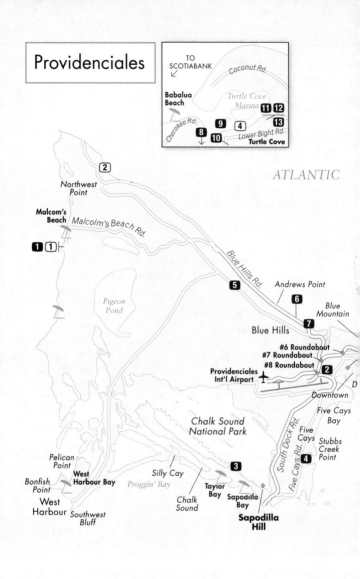

# Providenciales

**TO SCOTIABANK** ←

Coconut Rd.

**Babalua Beach**

*Turtle Cove Marina*

Cherokee Rd.

**9** **4** **11** **12**

**8** **13**

**10** Lower Bight Rd.

**Turtle Cove**

**2**

Northwest Point

**Malcom's Beach**

Malcom's Beach Rd.

**1** ①

Pigeon Pond

Blue Hills Rd.

**5**

Andrews Point

**6**

Blue Mountain

Blue Hills

**7**

#6 Roundabout
#7 Roundabout
#8 Roundabout

Providenciales Int'l Airport

**2**

Downtown

Five Cays Bay

Chalk Sound National Park

Five Cays

Stubbs Creek Point

South Dock Rd.

**4**

Pelican Point

**West Harbour Bay**

Bonfish Point

West Harbour

Southwest Bluff

Silly Cay

*Proggin' Bay*

Chalk Sound

**3**

Taylor Bay

Sapodilla Bay

**Sapodilla Hill**

Five Cays Rd.

*ATLANTIC*

**KEY**

⟋ *Beaches*
**1** *Restaurants*
① *Hotels*

0      2miles
0      2 km

OCEAN

Water Cay

Little Water Cay

Donna Cay

Half Moon Bay

Mangrove Cay

Pelican Beach

Crist Point

**15** **3**

Leeward

Provo Golf & Country Club

Governor's Rd.

Caicos Conch Farm

Princess Alexandra National Marine Park

**Grace Bay See Detail Map**

Grace Bay

Leeward Hwy.

Stubbs Cove

Thompson Cove

**#1 Roundabout**

Long Bay

Lower Bight Beach

**#3 Roundabout**

The Bight

**#2 Roundabout**

Leeward Hwy.

Long Bay

Long Bay Hwy.

Turks Island Passage

Turtle Cove See inset

**#5 Roundabout**

**14**

**Cheshire Hall**

**6**

Richmond Hills

**Graceway IGA**

Juba Point Salina

Venetian Rd.

**8**

**#4 Roundabout**

Turtle Tail Dr.

Juba Point

Discovery Bay

**5**

Turtle Tail

Cooper Jack Bight

Five Little Cays

Cooper Jack Point

---

**Hotels**

Amanyara, **1**

The Atrium, **3**

Harboour Club Villas, **5**

La Vista Azul, **6**

Northwest Point Resort, **2**

Turtle Cove Inn, **4**

**Restaurants**

Angela's Top o' the Cove, **8**

Baci Ristorante, **11**

Bugaloo's, **4**

Corner Café, **14**

Da Conch Shack, **6**

Fresh Bakery & Café, **15**

Greenbean, **13**

Hole in the Wall, **2**

Horse-Eye Jacks, **7**

Las Brisas, **3**

Magnolia Wine Bar & Restaurant, **10**

The Restaurant at Amanyara, **1**

Sharkbites Bar & Grill, **12**

Three Mary Queens, **5**

Tiki Hut, **9**

Ferries leave from Provo to North Caicos several times a day, and from there you can rent a car to explore Middle Caicos, though all these arrangements must be made in advance.

Contacts **Caribbean Cruisin'** ✉ *Walkin Marina, Leeward* ☎ *649/946–5406, 649/231–4191* ⊕ *www.tciferry.com.* **Salt Cay Ferry** ✉ *Salt Cay* ☎ *649/244–1407* ⊕ *www.turksandcaicoswhalewatching.com.*

It's possible to stay on Providenciales for a week without renting a car if you are willing to rely on very expensive taxis, a bicycle, or your own two feet. There are certainly parts of Grace Bay that are walkable, with many nearby restaurants and shops, and some tour operators will pick you up at your hotel or villa. But it's usually advisable to rent a car for at least a few days so you'll have the flexibility to explore independently. Driving is on the left, however (British style), so keep that in mind.

Signage for roads on Provo can be hard to come by, but locals use the island's eight roundabouts as their landmarks. Once you get a feel for those, driving around the island may not feel as daunting. All directions given are based off these roundabouts. *See the Providenciales map for more information on where these are.*

Here is a complete list:

1. Texaco (for Seven Stars)

2. Thomas Stubbs (for Beaches Resort)

3. IGA Graceway Supermarket

4. Felix Morley (for Venetian Road, Texaco)

5. Napa Auto Parts, Susie Turn (a tiny roundabout, so don't run through it)

6. Five Cays, Lime, First Caribbean Bank (no sign for this one)

7. Fuller Walker (for Blue Hills)

8. Walter Cox, South Dock Road (for the airport)

## TOP REASONS TO GO

**Grace Bay Beach.** The beach is the Turks and Caicos' biggest draw. The soft, powder-white sand with crystal-clear seas seems to go on for as far as the eye can see. Be warned: You will fall in love with this beach and want to come back and retire here.

**Snorkel, Scuba, and Snuba.** The world's third-largest reef system here makes for an underwater dream. Beginners and experts alike can snorkel right off the beach at Coral Gardens and Smith's Reef. The visibility is ideal, usually more than 100 feet. If you aren't a certified diver, Snuba is a choice for you; the tanks stay on the surface while you explore below.

**Fine Dining.** On quiet islands like Provo, dining is your nightlife. And while the food

is incredible across the island, what really stand out are the settings. Anocoana has what may be the best ambience in the entire Caribbean.

**Water Sports.** Turks and Caicos are all about the water, and not always what's below the surface. On Grace Bay you can parasail, ride a banana boat, sail a Hobie Cat, ride a kayak, or learn to windsurf. Long Bay Beach is the place to go kite surfing. Leeward Marina and the cays are great skiing and tubing areas.

**The Perfect Night Out.** At sunset, have a drink at Grace Bay Beach; end the night watching Mr. Blou sing under the stars at Mango Reef or Quiton Dean sing popular songs with a Caribbean twist.

# EXPLORING PROVIDENCIALES

While you may be quite content to enjoy the beaches and top-notch amenities of Provo's resorts, there are certainly plenty of activities beyond the resorts. Provo is a great starting point for island-hopping tours by sea or by air as well as fishing and diving trips. Resurfaced roads make for easy travel.

## GRACE BAY

The "hub" of the island is the stunning Grace Bay Beach. It lines the north shore on the island's Atlantic side. Grace Bay Road, which runs parallel to the beach a few blocks inland, is lined with many shops, restaurants, and resorts and has both sidewalks and streetlights. This area is where the majority of tourists stay (especially for their first visit to the island), and it's where all vacationers end up sooner or later.

## THE BIGHT

This beach area is popular for off-the-beach snorkeling and an even more popular Thursday night Fish Fry. It's hard to tell where the Bight starts and Grace Bay ends, so some consider it simply the "quiet end" of Grace Bay.

## TURTLE COVE

The Bight Beach also blends with the beach around Turtle Cove. Because this section of beach is rock, it's more popular for snorkeling. The popular Turtle Cove Marina is lined with excursion companies and also has a couple of popular restaurants, including Magnolia's and Tiki Hut.

## LEEWARD

An upscale residential area, Leeward is the eastward extension of Grace Bay. It also blends with Pelican Beach the farther it goes along. Although the sand is still smooth here, you can find a fair number of shells, including big conch shells, embedded in the sand. At the easternmost end of the area is Heaving Rock Marina, where the ferry to North Caicos is based.

FAMILY **Caicos Conch Farm.** More than 3 million conchs are farmed at this commercial operation on the northeast tip of Provo. It's a popular tourist attraction, too, with guided tours and a small gift shop selling conch-related souvenirs, jewelry, and freshwater pearls. You can even meet Jerry and Sally, the resident conchs that are brought out on demand. ✉ *Leeward-Going-Through, Leeward* ☎ *649/946–5330* ⊕ *www.caicosconchfarm. net/* ✎ *$12* ☺ *Weekdays 9–4, Sat. 9–2:30.*

## VENETIAN ROAD

Located behind the Graceway IGA supermarket on Leeward Highway, this major road leads to the beaches and mansions of Turtle Tail, including popular spots for flamingo-spotting.

## TURTLE TAIL

Located south of Graceway IGA supermarket on the highway in the middle of the island, there are isolated beaches and gorgeous mansions to see. If you like isolation, this is one of the quietest areas on the island and is the location of many vacation villas with stunning views of Caicos Banks.

## Providenciales in One Day

If you are doing a stopover in Provo on your way to another island, or if you don't want to rent a car for the duration of your trip, it's still worthwhile to rent a high-clearance vehicle and go around the island for a day. Start at Pelican Beach in search of empty conch shells. Then check out the Conch Farm, the only one in the world. While you're at the Conch Farm, say hello to Sally and Jerry, the resident conchs. You can also stop and see Cheshire Hill on your way to Chalk Sound. Chalk Sound is the island's one must-see. The water here is shallow and bright with small, mushroomlike islands in the middle, like a miniature Palau; the sight takes your breath away. If you want some beach time, check out Sapodilla Bay and Taylor Bay, where the waters are shallow for hundreds of yards, making them a child's dream. Take a ride to Malcolm's Beach on the Northwest Point, where just getting there is the adventure. Finish the afternoon at Blue Hills, where colorful buildings are the setting for a game of "slamming" dominos.

### DISCOVERY BAY

On the way to Turtle Tail, this pond is surrounded by houses and is the best place on the island to see flamingos. South Dock Road leads to gorgeous views of Chalk Sound, Sapodilla Bay, and Taylor Bay.

### DOWNTOWN

Although there are some businesses concentrated here, Downtown is primarily a commercial area near the airport that does not offer much for tourists. You can see ruins of an old plantation here.

**Cheshire Hall.** Standing eerily just west of downtown Provo are the remains of a circa-1700 cotton plantation owned by the Loyalist Thomas Stubbs. A trail weaves through the ruins, where a few interpretive signs tell the story of the island's doomed cotton industry, with little information about the plantation itself. A variety of local plants are also identified. The lack of context can be disappointing for history buffs; a visit to North Caicos Wades Green plantation or the Turks & Caicos National Museum could well prove a better fit. ⊠ *Leeward Hwy, behind Ace Hardware, Leeward* ☎ *649/941–5710 for National Trust* ⊕ *www.tcinationaltrust. org* ⊠ *$5* ⊙ *Mon.–Sat. 8:30–4:30 (guided tour required).*

## AIRPORT

The airport area is small and overcrowded, but expansion is in the works. Aside from the airport itself, there's nothing to attract tourists.

## FIVE CAYS

The biggest attraction in this relatively poor, working-class area behind the airport is the ever-popular Bugaloo's. Go on a Sunday afternoon for live music, when the whole island seems to turn up.

## CHALK SOUND

You will never ever lay eyes on more beautiful water. At the edge of the airport this "pond" has contrasting mushroom islands that really make the water appear to glow. Do not miss this national park.

**Chalk Sound National Park.** As you drive toward Sapodilla Bay on South Dock Road, on your right you will get glimpses of Chalk Sound. The water here is the brightest turquoise you'll ever see, and the mushroom-like tiny islands make the colors even bolder. There are a couple of places to stop for pictures, or you can enjoy lunch overlooking it at Las Brisas Restaurant. No matter how many times you see it, it still manages to take your breath away. ⊠ *Chalk Sound Rd., Chalk Sound.*

FAMILY **Sapodilla Hill.** On this cliff overlooking the secluded Sapodilla Bay, you can discover rocks carved with the names of shipwrecked sailors and dignitaries from TCI's maritime and colonial past. There are carvings on the rocks that some claim are secret codes and maps to hidden treasures; many have tried in vain to find these treasures. The hill is known by two other names, Osprey Rock and Splitting Rock. The less adventurous can see molds of the carvings at Provo's International Airport. It's best to go by boat with Captain Bill's Adventures, as cars in the parking area are occasionally broken into. ⊠ *Off South Dock Rd., west of South Dock, Chalk Sound.*

## Taxi Fares on Providenciales

Already expensive taxi fares on Providenciales went up in 2013. Rates are listed on a schedule, which is based on distance; nevertheless, newcomers may not know what to expect. Knowing approximate fares in advance may help you decide if you do want to rent a car. Just remember that all taxi fares are based on two people traveling and include two pieces of luggage each. Extra luggage is $4 per piece (golf bags $3 each), but grocery bags are free. Kids under 12 traveling with an adult add $6 each per trip. You pay 60¢ per minute to have a taxi wait for you, say at a grocery store. Here are some approximate fares (based on two people traveling together from the airport):

Turtle Cove: $16

Cable & Wireless: $16

Discovery Bay (for Graceway IGA or South Dock): $20

The Bight (for Coral Gardens or Reef Residences): $23

The Bight (for Beaches): $27

West Grace Bay (for Sibonné, Alexandra, Sands, Somerset, Point Grace, Villa Renaissance, Regent Grand, or Saltmills): $28

Mid Grace Bay (for Grace Bay Club, Seven Stars, Graceway Gourmet, Coco Bistro): $25

Grace Bay (for Ocean Club West, Caribbean Paradise Inn, Ports of Call): $35

Long Bay: $36

Upper Chalk Sound: $36

East Grace Bay (for Ocean Club, Tuscany, Royal West Indies, Club Med): $40

Leeward (Conch Farm, Marina): $43

Lower Chalk Sound, Silly Creek: $48

Northwest Point (for Amanyara): $86

## WEST HARBOUR

Caves, Osprey Rock, and treasure map pirate carvings makes this an enticing place to explore. On a secluded southwest part of the island, it's a long drive out, and the parking lot has had some break-ins. For now it's best to explore by boat.

## BLUE MOUNTAIN

Many gorgeous private villas with ocean views can be found here. The beaches are smaller and more private than those elsewhere on the island, and although it's in a central location, visitors staying here will require transportation to reach the best beaches.

## On a Budget in the TCI

If you would like to visit one of the world's most beautiful beaches but feel you can't afford this expensive destination, there are ways to save money in the Turks and Caicos and still have an enjoyable trip. Online agents Travelocity, Expedia, and Orbitz can often save you a few hundred dollars on a vacation package that combines airfare and hotel (and perhaps a car rental), but even better is the local website ⊕ *Turksand-CaicosReservations.tc*, which works with different resorts and can offer additional discounts, including free car rentals, spa treatments, and restaurant vouchers. Traveling during non-peak season, when many resorts offer free nights and extra perks, is another way to save. The discount season coincides with hurricane season (June through November), so consider purchasing travel insurance if you visit then. If you don't mind being a block or two from the beach, you can even save more.

Once on the island there are other ways to save. Most resort rooms and condos have refrigerators and microwaves, so you can stock up at the supermarket. Graceway IGA has awesome rotisserie chicken and prepared pasta and potato salads. Airlines will allow you to bring a cooler of food as long as perishables are frozen and vacuum sealed; despite airline charges for checked bags, this strategy could save you some money, especially on meat.

At restaurants, dinner might be more expensive than for the same entrée at lunchtime, so arrive 15 minutes before the switch-over and order from the lunch menu. Mango Reef offers four-course prix-fixe meals for a reasonable price. Every Wednesday night at Tiki Hut the $14 ribs are a bargain. You can also pick up food at Pizza Pizza and have a balcony picnic.

Even better, one of the island's top experiences is free: snorkeling off the beach at Coral Gardens.

A good source for events and specials is ⊕ *www.TCIenews.com*.

## BLUE HILLS

The "personality" of the island, this area populated with locals is west, beyond Grace Bay and Turtle Cove. The beachfront is lined with quirky beach shacks and colorful restaurants. It's a place to "chill" with water views, but no one ever swims here because there are better areas for beachcombing and hanging out on the sand.

## NORTHWEST POINT

The farthest point west on the island, it's a great scuba spot and has one secluded resort. Long stretches of beach are the primary attractions here (but only if you like solitude), and the beaches have a lot of sea grass, as well as being very windy and wavy.

# BEACHES

You want the best beaches in the world on vacation, don't you? That's what you will find in Provo. Everyone comes here for Grace Bay Beach, 12 uninterrupted miles (18 km) of clean sand with no rocks and unimaginably turquoise water, but you should not overlook Provo's other beaches, each with its own unique allure. You may find it hard to break away from Grace Bay, and although some beaches require some effort to reach, they will reward your effort. On the rare chance that north winds are creating waves on Grace Bay, you can always head to the other side of Provo for guaranteed calm and shallow waters. With no vendors on the beach to interrupt beach time, relieving stress has never been easier.

## GRACE BAY

★ **Fodor's**Choice **Grace Bay.** The 12-mile (18-km) sweeping stretch of ivory-white, powder-soft sand on Provo's north coast is simply breathtaking. It's home to migrating starfish as well as shallow snorkeling trails. The majority of Provo's beachfront resorts are along this shore, and it's the primary reason the Turks and Caicos is a world-class destination. **Amenities:** food and drink; parking (free); water sports. **Best for:** sunset; swimming; walking.

## THE BIGHT

**Lower Bight Beach.** Lower Bight Beach is often confused with Grace Bay Beach because it seems to blend right into it. Although the beach is gorgeous, it gets rocky here. It also has the best off-the-beach snorkeling—not just in Provo, but possibly the Caribbean. **Amenities:** food and drink; parking (free). **Best for:** snorkeling; walking. ⊠ *Lower Bight Rd., The Bight.*

## LEEWARD

**Pelican Beach.** Pelican Beach has the best souvenirs—huge, empty conch shells. Chances are you'll be the only one on this beautiful strand. Because of offshore dredging during the last couple of years, the water is not as crystal-clear as at Grace Bay, but it's an even brighter turquoise. **Amenities:** parking (free). **Best for:** solitude; walking. ⊠ *Sandpiper Ave., Leeward* ✛ *On Grace Bay Rd. at Seven Stars, keep straight on Grace Bay Rd. until you pass an unmanned gatehouse. At the big circle take your first left, Sandpiper Ave. At the small roundabout take a left until road ends and park. On the beach it blends with Leeward Beach and Grace Bay on the left, on the right walk around to Pelican Beach.*

## BIG WATER CAY

★ **Fodor's**Choice **Half Moon Bay.** This natural ribbon of sand links two uninhabited cays; it's only inches above the sparkling turquoise waters and one of the most gorgeous beaches on the island. There are limestone cliffs to explore as well as small, sandy coves; there's even a small wreck offshore for snorkeling. It's only a short boat ride away from Provo, and most of the island's tour companies run excursions here or simply offer a beach drop-off. These companies include Silver Deep and Caicos Dream Tours *(⇨ Boating and Sailing, in Sports and the Outdoors).* **Amenities:** none. **Best for:** solitude; snorkeling; swimming; walking. ⊕ *Accessible only by boat, 15 mins from Leeward Marina.*

## LONG BAY

**Long Bay.** Long Bay is where the sports are. An excellent beach for horseback riding, it's also popular with kite-surfers. If you want to swim here, wear water shoes, as there are many conch shells half buried in the sand. Excursion companies will bring equipment to the beach for you because there are no concessions here of any kind. **Amenities:** parking (free). **Best for:** walking; windsurfing; kitesurfing. ⊠ *Long Bay Rd., Long Bay* ✛ *On Leeward Hwy., pass roundabout #1, Texaco and Seven Stars, staying straight on hwy. Take a right at Shore Club entrance. When road ends, take a right then an immediate left for public parking.*

## CHALK SOUND

**Sapodilla Bay.** The best of the many secluded beaches and pristine sands around Provo can be found at this peaceful quarter-mile cove protected by Sapodilla Hill. The soft strand here is lapped by calm waves, and yachts and small boats move with the gentle tide. During low tide, little sandbar "islands" form—they're great for a beach chair. **Amenities:** parking (free). **Best for:** walking. ⊠ *End of South Dock Rd., North of South Dock, Chalk Sound* ⊹ *From Leeward Hwy. take roundabout #6 towards Five Cays (there's no marking but there is a First Caribbean Bank in the corner). Follow until almost the end, past a small police station. Take a right at Chalk Sound Rd. First dirt road on left leads to a small parking area.*

**Taylor Bay.** Taylor Bay is shallow for hundreds of yards, making it a perfect place for a private picnic or sunset wedding. Kids become giddy at this beach; they can play in a huge area of chest-high water, and parents don't have to worry about dangerous drop-offs. The beach also offers gorgeous views for the many villas here. **Amenities:** none. **Best for:** solitude; swimming. ⊠ *Sunset Dr., Chalk Sound* ⊹ *From Leeward Hwy., take roundabout #6 towards Five Cays (there's no marking but there is a First Caribbean Bank in the corner). Follow the road until almost the end, past a small police station. Take a right on Chalk Sound Rd. Take left at Ocean Point Dr. and park next to entrance that has big boulders blocking a sand path. Follow this path to beach.*

GLOWWORMS. If you're here on the fourth and fifth days after a full moon, you might get to see glowworms. The phenomenon occurs when fluorescent worms mate, then glow in the water like stars twinkling at dusk. The worms will do their dance for about an hour. Sadly, a vibrant phosphorescent show is not guaranteed; some months offer tons of little "stars" in the water; some months are duds with only a few. The best places to view them from land are around the Caicos Banks and Chalk Sound residential neighborhoods. Better yet, see them from an excursion boat.

## NORTHWEST POINT

**Malcolm's Beach.** It's one of the most stunning beaches you'll ever see, but you'll need a high-clearance vehicle to reach it. Bring your own food and drinks, because it doesn't have any facilities or food service unless you have made a reservation to eat at the very expensive Amanyara resort. There have been reports of break-ins at the parking lot in years past, so it's best to not keep any valuables in your car. From Malcolm's parking lot, for the best beach area, walk towards Amanyara, where there are no boulders in the water. **Amenities:** parking (free). **Best for:** solitude; swimming; walking. ✉ *Malcolm's Beach Rd., beyond the Amanyara turnoff, Northwest Point* ✛ *On Leeward Hwy., take Fuller Walken roundabout towards Blue Hills. Keep following the road after it turns into rolled packed sand. Take the 2nd unpaved road on the left. Follow road until the end, which takes about 20 mins. There is a rough patch that requires caution.*

## WEST HARBOUR

**West Harbour Bay.** This is about as isolated as it gets on Provo. West Bay has long stretches of beaches to walk and explore, and there's no other person in sight for hours. Occasionally Captain Bill's Outback Adventure excursion stops here and explores the nearby pirate caves. Not only can you find big red starfish in the water here, but you might find a buried pirate's treasure if you correctly interpret the "maps" in the rock carvings. ⚠ **We can only recommend going by boat excursion, as there have been persistent break-ins at the parking lot.** Amenities: none. Best for: solitude; walking. ✉ *West Harbour.*

# WHERE TO EAT

Food choices on Provo are numerous, even for picky eaters. With more than dozens of restaurants to choose from, food choices run the gamut. Expats from around the world have opened restaurants with Moroccan, Thai, Spanish, and Indian themes. You'll find everything from small beach shacks with the freshest seafood right off the boats to elegant restaurants with extensive wine lists. Most of the restaurants that cater to tourists offer numerous choices, with a little bit of everything on the menu. Don't like seafood? Have chicken or beef. Don't like spice? Ask for the tamer version. Vegetarian? Need kid-friendly food? Feel free to ask for something that's not on the menu; most of the island's chefs will try to accommodate requests. Some restaurants will also set up a table on the beach surrounded by tiki torches for that special romantic dinner. Restaurants on Provo are generally upscale and expensive; you will find no fast-food or other chains here.

There are excellent caterers on the island, too. You can have Kissing Fish Catering pack a picnic lunch or cater a party on the beach.

You can spot the island's Caribbean influence everywhere. Local food is heavy on seafood, usually the catch of the day right off local boats, including lobster during the season that runs from August through March. It is illegal for restaurants to serve lobster out of season, so you will not find it on local menus from April to July. The best local food on the island is conch, which you will find everywhere prepared in many different ways. You may find it raw in a salad, as fried conch fingers, in spicy conch fritters, or in hearty conch chowder. It is often a part of fresh seafood specials, with colorful presentation and a tangy dose of spice.

Some restaurants do close during slow season, with dates fluctuating yearly—usually closings are from late August through late October. On the rare rainy day—or an unusually hot day—there are even a few indoor restaurants with air-conditioning, as noted in the individual reviews.

Pick up a free copy of *Where When How's Dining Guide*, which you can find all over the island; it contains menus, websites, and pictures of all the restaurants.

### RESTAURANT PRICES
*Prices in the restaurant reviews are the average cost of a main course at dinner or, if dinner is not served, at lunch; taxes and service charges are generally included.*

## GRACE BAY

**$$$$** ✕**Anacaona.** *Mediterranean.* At Grace Bay Club, this thatch-roofed restaurant has the best setting in the Turks and Caicos, and perhaps in the entire Caribbean. Despite its elite clientele and high prices, the restaurant continues to offer a memorable dining experience minus any formality and attitude (and minus the air-conditioning). That said, children under 12 are not allowed, and long pants and collared shirts are required for men. Oil lamps on the tables, gently revolving ceiling fans, and the murmur of the trade winds add to the Edenic environment. The entrancing ocean views and the careful service make this an ideal choice when you want to be pampered. The kitchen uses the island's bountiful seafood and fresh produce to craft healthy, Mediterranean-influenced cuisine. It's a good thing the setting is amazing, though; the portions are tiny for what you pay. ⑤ *Average main: $40* ✉ *Grace Bay Club, Grace Bay Circle Rd., Grace Bay* ☎ *649/946–5050* ⊕ *www.gracebayresorts.com/gracebayclub* ⚓ *Reservations essential* ⊙ *Closed Sept. No lunch.*

★ **Fodor's**Choice ✕ **Bay Bistro.** *International.* You simply can't eat
**$$$$** any closer to the beach than here, the only restaurant in all of
FAMILY Provo to be built directly on the sand. You dine on a covered porch (or on one of three individual platforms) surrounded by palm trees and the sound of lapping waves. The spring-roll appetizer is delicious, and the oven-roasted chicken is the best on the island. At the very popular weekend brunch, which includes such favorites as eggs Benedict with mimosas (included), lines can be long if you don't have a reservation. Around the time of the full moon, ask about the memorable beach barbecue: all-you-can-eat ribs, pig roast, and bonfire on the sand. ⑤ *Average main: $31* ✉ *Sibonné Beach Hotel, Princess Dr., Grace Bay* ☎ *649/946–5396* ⊕ *sibonne.com/grace-bay-bistro* ⚓ *Reservations essential.*

**$$$** ✕ **Bella Luna Ristorante.** *Italian.* For old-fashioned Italian food just like you can get at home, where pasta is the side dish, this is your best bet on Provo. The restaurant, which is a converted private house, is peaceful. You can also sit out in the gardens, which are threaded with lighted paths at night. Veal, fish, and chicken dishes are made with fresh herbs and wine-cream sauces, olive oil, and lemon butter. The best dish on the menu is the chicken sautéed with red peppers in a demi-glace flamed with cognac. If lobster Fra Diavolo is not on the menu, ask for it. But be warned, it's hot. ⑤ *Average main: $27* ✉ *The Glass House, Grace Bay Rd., Grace Bay* ☎ *649/946–5214* ⊙ *Closed Sun. No lunch.*

ROMANCE ON THE BEACH. **What more romantic way to celebrate a special occasion than with a terrific dinner directly on the beach? Several Provo restaurants will set a table on the shoreline, complete with tiki torches, candles, and tablecloths. Anacaona, Bay Bistro, and Kissing Fish Catering are a few of the places to turn for a special occasion. The beach is also a great setting for a marriage proposal.**

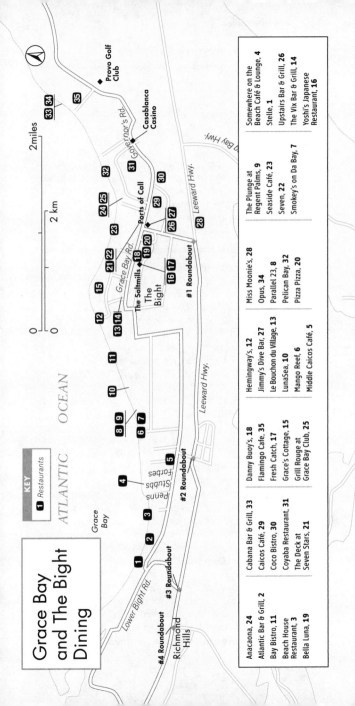

# Grace Bay and The Bight Dining

**KEY**

**1** Restaurants

ATLANTIC OCEAN

Grace Bay

Penns
Stubbs
Forbes

Richmond Hills

#4 Roundabout
#3 Roundabout
#2 Roundabout
#1 Roundabout

Lower Bight Rd.
Leeward Hwy.
Grace Bay Rd.
Governor's Rd.
Leeward Hwy.
Bay Hwy.

The Saltmills
The Bight
Ports of Call

Provo Golf Club
Casablanca Casino

2 miles
2 km

Anacaona, **24**
Atlantic Bar & Grill, **2**
Bay Bistro, **11**
Beach House Restaurant, **3**
Bella Luna, **19**

Cabana Bar & Grill, **33**
Caicos Café, **29**
Coco Bistro, **30**
Coyaba Restaurant, **31**
The Deck at Seven Stars, **21**

Danny Buoy's, **18**
Flamingo Cafe, **35**
Fresh Catch, **17**
Grace's Cottage, **15**
Grill Rouge at Grace Bay Club, **25**

Hemingway's, **12**
Jimmy's Dive Bar, **27**
Le Bouchon du Village, **13**
LunaSea, **10**
Mango Reef, **6**
Middle Caicos Café, **5**

Miss Moonie's, **28**
Opus, **34**
Parallel 23, **8**
Pelican Bay, **32**
Pizza Pizza, **20**

The Plunge at Regent Palms, **9**
Seaside Café, **23**
Seven, **22**
Smokey's on Da Bay, **7**

Somewhere on the Beach Café & Lounge, **4**
Stelle, **1**
Upstairs Bar & Grill, **26**
The Vix Bar & Grill, **14**
Yoshi's Japanese Restaurant, **16**

## Provo's Thursday Fish Fry

On Thursday nights at the Bight Park (which is next to the beach), you can taste food offerings from multiple restaurants in one place. Locals and tourists gather alike for the live music and great ambience. The smells from the grills will keep you hungry, and it's a great spot to compare who makes the best local foods. Upstairs Bar and Grill, Hole in the Wall, Smokey's on Da Bay, Miss Moonies, and Middle Caicos Cafe are just a few of the weekly participants. It's fun for the whole family, and the convenient location means that you don't have to leave the main tourist area to try some of the best local food.

$$ ✕ **Cabana Bar & Grill.** *American.* Cabana's a great option if you're looking for a quick lunch with a view of the beautiful beach just steps away. The food is good but unexciting, including such basic fare as hamburgers and wraps. The menu also includes Wednesday-night smoked snapper, chicken, and ribs; and Friday-night fish, chicken, or steak barbecue. Nightly happy hours and live music Monday and Thursday make this a prime place at sunset, too. ⑤ *Average main: $15* ⊠ *Ocean Club, Grace Bay Rd., Grace Bay* ☎ *649/946–5880* ⬟ *Reservations not accepted.*

$$$ ✕ **Caicos Café.** *Italian.* At what's probably the most popular restaurant with locals, the island dishes come with an Italian twist. The bruschetta that everyone gets at the start of the meal is delicious enough that you may ask for seconds, and the bread is baked fresh every day at the bakery next door. Blackened fish and jerk chicken on top of pasta are popular, but we think that ravioli with cream sauce is the tastiest dish. On windy nights, the inland setting offers protection from the breezes. Be sure to wear bug spray at night. ⑤ *Average main: $30* ⊠ *Caicos Café Plaza, Grace Bay Rd., Grace Bay* ☎ *649/946–5278* ⬟ *caicoscafe@tciway.tc* ⊗ *Closed Sun.*

★ **Fodor'sChoice** ✕ **Coco Bistro.** *International.* With tables under
$$$$ palm trees, Coco Bistro has a divine setting, and the food is just as good. Though not directly on the beach, the location under the tropical tree grove still reminds you that you are on vacation. Main courses are complemented by both French flourishes (served au poivre, for example) and West Indian (such as with mango chutney) and are accom-

panied by fried plantains and mango slaw to maintain a Caribbean flair. Consider conch soup, soft-shell-crab tempura, and sun-dried tomato pasta from the internationally influenced menu. Do not miss this restaurant, it is the best of the best on the island. ■TIP→ **Make reservations at least one week ahead during nonpeak season, two to three weeks ahead in peak season, as this is the most popular restaurant on island.** Ⓢ *Average main: $40* ⊠ *Grace Bay Rd., Grace Bay* ☎ *649/946–5369* ⊕ *www.CocoBistro.tc* ⌕ *Reservations essential* ⊘ *Closed Mon. No lunch.*

★ **Fodor's**Choice ✕**Coyaba Restaurant.** *International.* Directly
**$$$$** behind Grace Bay Club at Caribbean Paradise Inn, this posh restaurant is in a palm-fringed setting. The nostalgic favorites here are served with tempting twists in conversation-piece crockery. Chef Paul Newman uses his culinary expertise for the daily-changing main courses, which include exquisitely presented dishes such as crispy, whole, yellow snapper fried in Thai spices. One standout is lobster Thermidor in a Dijon-mushroom cream sauce. You may want to try several different appetizers instead of an entrée for dinner; guava-and-tamarind barbecue ribs and coconut-shrimp tempura are two good choices if you go that route. If you enjoy creative menus, this is the place for you. Coyaba keeps the resident expat crowd happy with traditional favorites such as lemon meringue pie, albeit with his own tropical twist. Don't skip dessert; Paul makes incredible chocolate fondant. Ⓢ *Average main: $34* ⊠ *Caribbean Paradise Inn, Bonaventure Crescent, off Grace Bay Rd., Grace Bay* ☎ *649/946–5186* ⊕ *www. coyabarestaurant.com* ⌕ *Reservations essential* ⊘ *Closed Tues. No lunch.*

**$$** ✕**Danny Buoy's.** *Irish.* A true local watering hole, this bar always has a mix of locals and vacationers. It's your typical pub, where you can watch your favorite sport no matter what part of the world you're from, but a fair number of people come here not only to drink but to dine on traditional Irish favorites such as fish-and-chips and potpies. Especially on weekends, this is one of the few places with some nightlife, which includes karaoke and live music, and you will always find it open late. Ⓢ *Average main: $20* ⊠ *Grace Bay Rd., next to the Saltmills, Grace Bay* ☎ *649/946–5921* ⊕ *www.dannybuoys.com* ⌕ *Reservations not accepted.*

**$$$** ✕**The Deck at Seven Stars.** *Eclectic.* It's hard to think of a more alluring setting than this deck on the dunes overlooking the ocean, part of the posh Seven Stars resort. Tiki torches, fire pits, and awnings lend plenty of chic to this otherwise much more casual sister to the property's more formal restaurant, Seven. Nosh on small plates, or consider one of the fine lobster or pasta dishes. Go on a Thursday or Saturday night when there's live music, or on Sunday for the sunset beach barbecue with live music. ⑤ *Average main: $22* ⊠ *Seven Stars Resort, Grace Bay Rd., Grace Bay* ☎ *649/339–3777* ⊕ *www.sevenstarsgracebay.com.*

$$ ✕ **Flamingo Cafe.** *Caribbean.* Offering local fare in the middle of the main tourist area at reasonable prices, this gorgeous, casual restaurant is a local favorite. The setting is terrific under a porch with views of the beach, at the Cultural Center next to Club Med, so you can do some light local shopping, too. Island favorites, including curry grouper with coconut sauce, jerk chicken with peas and rice, and tangy homemade barbecue ribs are cooked on open charcoal flame. This is the best place to be on New Year's Eve, when there's a bonfire beach barbecue that offers a beachside venue for myriad fireworks displays. ■TIP→ **This restaurant is widely known by the owner's name and not by the official name, so if asking directions, ask for "Rickie's."** ⑤ *Average main: $18* ⊠ *Cultural Center, Grace Bay Rd., Grace Bay* ☎ *649/242–7545* ✉ *flamingo_cafe@hotmail.com.*

$ ✕ **Fresh Catch.** *Seafood.* This small, very casual local restaurant serves primarily seafood that is brought in daily straight from the boats. Landlubbers can also order chicken, but that's about it. The place is blissfully air-conditioned but offers few other frills. You can also buy fresh fish and lobster by the pound to take back and cook at your resort or villa, so it's no longer necessary to drive all the way to Five Cays to get fresh seafood. But you can't get dinner because the place closes by 6 pm. ⑤ *Average main: $12* ⊠ *Saltmills Plaza, Grace Bay Rd., Unit 6, Grace Bay* ☎ *649/243–3167* ⊗ *Closed Sun. No dinner.*

$$$$ ✕ **Grace's Cottage.** *International.* At one of the prettiest dining settings on Provo, the tables are artfully set under wrought-iron cottage-style gazebos and around the wraparound veranda, which skirts the gingerbread-covered main building. The tangy and exciting entrées may include lobster lasagna with diced veggies or melt-in-your-mouth grilled beef tenderloin with truffle fries. The portions are small, but the quality is high. You might want to end with the mango-infused cheesecake because, after all, you're at the beach. Service is impeccable (ladies are given a small stool so that their purses do not touch the ground). On Tuesday nights, live music adds to the good vibes. ⑤ *Average*

## Groceries on Provo

Provo offers many of the conveniences of home, but there is only one large supermarket, Graceway IGA, that has a full-service deli and bakery. It's a huge supermarket like you would find at home, with popular American, Canadian, and British brands. But sticker shock may set in when you see that prices are usually 50% more than what you would pay at home. The store also sells everything you need for the beach, from suntan lotion to beach chairs and floats. It is centrally located in Discovery Bay, so that if you get tired of eating out and spending lots of money, you will have a wonderful alternative. There are also smaller markets such as Quality Supermarket and Island Pride that offer similar products on a smaller scale. But Graceway Gourmet, a smaller offshoot of Graceway IGA, offers many gourmet and organic foods—it's across from Seven Stars Resort—within walking distance of most resorts on Grace Bay Road. If you're shopping on a smaller scale, some resorts have small convenience stores for staples such as milk, snacks, and coffee. The best places for ice are the three real supermarkets.

*main: $40* ✉ *Point Grace, Off Grace Bay Rd., Grace Bay* ☎ *649/946–5096* ⊕ *www.pointgrace.com* ⚓ *Reservations essential* ⊘ *No lunch.*

**$$$** ✕**Grill Rouge at Grace Bay Club.** *American.* The Grill's setting is gorgeous, with a wooden trellis, banquettes, and fire pits set in the sand under scattered awnings. The menu is more casual than that of Anacaona (also at the Grace Bay Club), with typical grill fare such as hamburgers and chicken and fish sandwiches; and it's also open for lunch. If you want something more substantial, you can also order from Anacaona's menu. Note that service can be extremely slow. ⓢ *Average main: $29* ✉ *Villas at Grace Bay Club, Bonaventure Crescent, Grace Bay* ☎ *649/946–5050.*

**$$$** ✕**Hemingway's.** *Eclectic.* The casual and gorgeous setting, with a patio and deck offering views of Grace Bay, makes this one of the most popular tourist restaurants. At lunch don't miss the best fish tacos, with mango chutney. For dinner there is an excellent kids' menu and something for everyone, including vegetarians. Order the popular "Old Man of the Sea," which features the freshest fish of the day. It's known for great sauces such as the wine reduction for the filet mignon, the creole for fish dishes, and a delicious curry for chicken. If you're on a budget, go right before 6 pm, when you can still order the less expensive lunch menu items. On Monday NaDa sings while you dine, Thursday and Friday nights there's additional live music that adds to the ambience. ⑤ *Average main: $25* ✉ *The Sands at Grace Bay, Grace Bay Rd., Grace Bay* ☎ *649/946–5199.*

**$$** ✕ **Jimmy's Dive Bar.** *American.* A casual option that's not hard on the wallet, this restaurant is a terrific choice for breakfast. Later in the day, expect mostly hamburgers and sandwiches, but if you're craving something more, you can get pasta, lobster (in season), and a huge 24-ounce porterhouse steak. It's in a great spot for people-watching, and it's open later than other restaurants, so if you're coming off a late flight, this is a good bet for food or just a lively spot to meet other vacationers. Expect this to live up to its name—it's truly a dive. ⑤ *Average main: $15* ✉ *Ports of Call, Grace Bay Rd., Grace Bay* ☎ *No phone* ⚏ *Reservations not accepted.*

**$$** ✕ **Le Bouchon du Village.** *Bistro.* If you close your eyes, the aromas and tastes you will experience at this new bistro in Regent Village may make you think that you're sitting in a Parisian bistro. Food is exactly what you would expect, including escargot, steak au poivre with frites, and cheese boards. Unescapable conch ceviche adds island flair to the otherwise French menu, which is written on a chalkboard. The quality rivals fine dining available elsewhere in Provo without the price tag. Although reservations are not needed, this place is extremely popular with the locals for dinner. The restaurant is operated by the original owners of Caicos Cafe, who have a loyal following for a reason. ⑤ *Average main: $18* ✉ *Regent Village, Grace Bay Rd., Grace Bay* ☎ *649/946–5234* ⊙ *Closed Sun.*

**$$** ✕ **LunaSea Pool Bar and Grill.** *American.* At the Somerset Resort, in a gazebo with views of the gorgeous colors of Grace Bay Beach, you'll think you're truly having your burger in paradise. Other lunch offerings include hot dogs, fish-and-chips, and an outstanding chicken wrap with pecans and apples. Ask the chef if he's willing to make satay chicken with peanut sauce; it is the best lunch on the island. The bartender makes exotic tropical martinis, such as the mangotini, that you can sip by the pool. The bar will even bring buckets of beer to you on the beach, so you never have to leave your little patch of sand. ⑤ *Average main: $15* ✉ *The Somerset Resort on Grace Bay, Princess Dr., Grace Bay* ☎ *649/946–5900* ⊕ *thesomerset.com* ⚏ *Reservations not accepted* ⊙ *No dinner.*

**$** ✕**Miss Moonies.** *Deli.* When you take a 24-hour convenience store and add a gorgeous pool courtyard setting you get something completely different for Provo. The deli here has prepared foods, including ribs, or you can have sandwiches made to go. If you don't feel like going, then simply sit inside or outside by the pool. No matter when you're hungry, you can get breakfast (all day and night) or just a smoothie. The store also sells snacks and other staples for those late night munchies. During holidays concerts are set up across the street on a stage (these can go on all night). Miss Moonie also has a booth every Thursday at the Fish Fry at the Bight. ⑤ *Average main: $6* ✉ *Leeward Hwy. Grace Bay* ☎ *649/941–6664.*

**$$$** ✕**Mango Reef.** *Eclectic.* This is arguably the most popular restaurant of vacationers on the island. It's reasonably priced by Provo standards and has an ever-popular three-course dinner for $42. Although the food can be inconsistent, try the lobster ravioli, which is reliably quite good. Try to go on a Tuesday or Friday night, when NaDa performs easy-listening tunes while you dine (check ahead for music schedule). Make reservations on the deck so you can watch sunsets at the beach while you dine. ⑤ *Average main: $23* ✉ *The Alexandra Resort, Princess Rd., Grace Bay* ☎ *649/946–8200* ⊕ *www.mangoreef.com.*

**$$$** ✕**Opus.** *International.* If you arrive in Provo on a late-evening flight, you still have a chance for fine dining. This is one of the few restaurants on the island open until 11 pm. A beautifully landscaped patio makes a quietly elegant setting. The menu here emphasizes meat: a fire-grilled rib-eye steak with cognac-cream sauce, filet mignon with horseradish demi-glace, and pork chops with salsa. If you want fish, order one of the daily specials. The best part of the meal is dessert; who can pass up the chocolate brownies with cheesecake swirl? Make sure to have a nightcap at the bar; it gets lively around 10. ⑤ *Average main: $27* ✉ *Ocean Club, Grace Bay Rd., Grace Bay* ☎ *649/946–5885* ⊕ *www.opustci.com* ☽ *Closed Mon. No lunch.*

**$$$$** ✕**Parallel 23.** *Seafood.* The international menu at this upscale spot focuses on fish and seafood, though foie gras remains one of the menu's highlights, as well as a four-way surprise Conch appetizer and sea bass served on Champagne cabbage. The covered porch looks into a courtyard and gives you the feeling that you're dining on the porch of a majestic plantation. Offerings also include the best vegetarian and vegan food on the island. Two servers assigned to each table ensure good service, and Chef Lauren is one of the best cooks on the island. Food presentation is artful, using beautiful plates of different sizes. Although it's dimly lighted, keep an eye out for celebrities. ⑤ *Average main: $38* ⊠ *Regent Palms Resort, Regent St., Grace Bay* ☎ *649/946–8666* ⚑ *Reservations essential* ☉ *No lunch.*

$$$ ✕ **Pelican Bay.** *International.* The dining here is in an airy room, with French doors that lead to a breezy patio. The capable chef, Peter Redstone, uses local ingredients to create such internationally influenced dishes as Greek salad, Thai-spiced lobster cakes with grilled-corn-and-tomato jam, and sesame-crusted Atlantic salmon with a lemongrass beurre blanc. An entire menu of dishes is made with locally caught lobster, including lobster potpie with a side of truffle fries, and lobster tail in a jerk sauce finished with Guinness beer. Fridays feature a beachside pig roast, while on Sunday there's a jerk chicken fiesta buffet with live entertainment. ⑤ *Average main: $22* ⊠ *Royal West Indies Resort, Bonaventure Crescent, Grace Bay* ☎ *649/941–2365* ⊕ *www.pelicanbaytci.com.*

$$ ✕ **Pizza Pizza.** *Pizza.* Sometimes you just don't want to dress up to go out. And sometimes it's your wallet that needs a vacation. Here is your answer. The menu includes all the standard toppings, including pepperoni, onions, green peppers, and olives, but there are also some more exotic options like conch, mussels, clams, and squid. In addition to good pizza, don't forget excellent lasagna; not only is it tasty, but you'll have enough left over for lunch the next day. You can either pick up your food or have it delivered for a balcony picnic. ⑤ *Average main: $20* ⊠ *Grace Bay Plaza, Grace Bay Rd., Grace Bay* ☎ *649/941–8010.*

$$$$ ✕ **The Plunge at Regent Palms.** *American.* This sunken restaurant by the pool is colorful, vibrant, and a great spot for people-watching. You can choose to sit in a long banquette with colorful pillows, at the bar, or on swim-up tables built right into the pool, so you can eat in your swimsuit. The casual menu has sandwiches, hamburgers, and pizza, and a very good chicken wrap with a creamy sauce; there are more upscale options for dinner. Be prepared to pay, though; even tea refills will cost you. ⑤ *Average main: $34* ⊠ *Regent Palms, Regent St., Grace Bay* ☎ *649/946–8666.*

$ ✕ **Seaside Café.** *American.* The casual restaurant at Ocean Club West is a clone of the Cabana Bar & Grill at the Ocean Club. The usual casual fare, including hamburgers, salads, and wraps, can be eaten with a view of Grace Bay Beach all day long and into the night. Head to the deck to get closer to the beach. ⑤ *Average main: $15* ⊠ *Ocean Club West, Grace Bay Rd., Grace Bay* ☎ *649/946–5880* ⊕ *oceanclubresorts.com.*

**$$$$** ✕ **Seven.** *International.* Elegant and beautiful, this swanky restaurant at Seven Stars Resort is one of only a few on the island with air-conditioning; there's also a covered patio with attractive outdoor seating that's ideal on pleasant evenings. Expect innovative, artfully prepared food here—you might choose sea scallops with horseradish cream and Iberico ham to start, and jerk-braised pork belly or house-made stone-crab ravioli among the entrées. The lobster, among the best on the island, is served with a delicious rum-butter sauce. Meals are served with a variety of flavorful salts from Salt Cay. ⑤ *Average main: $32* ✉ *Seven Stars Resort, Grace Bay Rd., Grace Bay* ☎ *649/941–7777* ⊕ *www.sevenstarsgracebay.com.*

**$$** ✕ **Smokey's on Da Bay.** *Caribbean.* Smokey has been popular regardless of where he was located on the island, and he's been all over the island. He was so successful he took his money, traveled, gambled, entertained, and now he's back. People flock for fantastic ribs and authentic rice and peas, making his one of the best local places to eat. A handy location behind Alexandra Resort means it's easier for tourists and locals to mingle—and perhaps play a game of slamming dominoes. One of a few indoor restaurants on the island means the air-conditioning and roof gives you a break from heat or rain. During the Friday happy hour fish fry there's live music in the courtyard. What you won't find is a menu; just ask what's cooking. Your alcohol choices include only beer and rum punch. ⑤ *Average main: $18* ✉ *Behind Alexandra Resort, Grace Bay* ☎ *649/247–2935* ⊟ *No credit cards.*

**$$** ✕ **Upstairs Bar & Grill.** *American.* This new restaurant, formerly Calico Jack's, has new owners and a completely new concept. Within walking distance from numerous resorts and easier on the wallet than most other nearby restaurants in the heart of Grace Bay, Upstairs can still compete with the more expensive spots when it comes to taste. Casual burgers, wings, and ribs offer what is, for some, a welcome break from all the fine dining; the risotto and pizzas on the grill are standouts. ⑤ *Average main: $17* ✉ *Ports of Call Shopping Center, Grace Bay Rd., Grace Bay* ☎ *649/941–8914* ⊕ *upstairsbarandgrill.com* ⚉ *Reservations not accepted.*

**$$$$** ✕ **The Vix Bar & Grill.** *Eclectic.* The ambience at this upscale, outdoor café, which is in a pretty courtyard at Regent Village, is relaxed and perfect for people-watching. Produce is fresh, steaks are certified dry-Angus, and seafood is local. Hoisin-roasted duck has a hint of Asian flavor, the rib eye is flame-grilled, and chicken pâté is marinated in local

## Weekly Restaurant Happenings

**CLOSE UP**

Many of Provo's restaurants have weekly specials you can count on. Here are some of our favorites. The website ⊕ *tcienews.com* can keep you up-to-date on any changes.

On Tuesday, Da Conch shack has $10.99 jerk chicken.

Wednesday night is hopping at Tiki Hut, which has a $14 rib special. The restaurant only takes reservations for five or more people, so you'll need to arrive early, but even then be prepared to wait because it's a popular night.

On Thursday night at Hemingway's, mellow live bands play Caribbean-accented versions of popular songs, offering an excellent opportunity for the kids to dance while you dine. At Somewhere On the Beach at Coral Gardens, Just plays reggae music. Da Conch Shack brings in live bands on Thursday.

On Friday night, start early at Mango Reef with live music, followed by a DJ at the Gansevoort.

On Saturday night Opus has live music with Correy Forbes.

On Sunday you can have a great brunch at Bay Bistro; it doesn't offer a traditional buffet, but the setting is great, as are the included mimosas. If you happen upon a full moon, do not miss Bay Bistro's beach barbecue bonfire.

Sunday night is magical at Seven Stars, where there's a barbecue on the beach with live music. Wiggling your toes in the sand while you eat is priceless.

---

Bamberra Rum. Preparations and presentation are sophisticated. There are also weekly specials, including British pub fare on Thursday. Weekend brunch is popular. Local expats often drop in later at night. ⑤ *Average main: $32* ⊠ *Regent Village, Regent St., Grace Bay* ☎ *649/941–4144* ⊕ *www.thevix.com.*

$$ ✕ **Yoshi's Japanese Restaurant.** *Japanese.* This very good destination for Japanese food is also one of the few restaurants with indoor, air-conditioned seating. The menu here is reasonably priced, and includes fresh sushi and basics like chicken teriyaki as well as local conch. The house salad with ginger dressing and the appetizer spring rolls are a delight. If you don't want to stay indoors, it's a great place to sit outside and people-watch, too. ⑤ *Average main: $20* ⊠ *Saltmills Plaza, Grace Bay Rd., Grace Bay* ☎ *649/941–3374* ⊕ *yoshissushi.net* ⊘ *No lunch Sun.*

## THE BIGHT

**$$$** ✕ **Atlantic Bar & Grill.** *American.* What sets this casual restaurant apart from the rest is that all the entrées are cooked on outdoor grills within view. If you aren't hungry when you arrive, just wait until you smell the grilled meats; the aromas alone will make you salivate. Fish, lamb, and steaks are best simply grilled, but ask for extra sauce; there usually isn't enough. The restaurant can also cater private dinners on the beach and other events. ⑤ *Average main: $25* ⊠ *The West Bay Club, Lower Bight Rd., The Bight* ☎ *649/946–8550* ⊕ *www.thewestbayclub.com.*

**$$$$** ✕ **Beach House Restaurant.** *Eclectic.* "From farm to table" is a new concept for Provo, but this exciting restaurant by chef Eric Vernice pairs French traditions with Caribbean ingredients to great effect. The regular menu features oven-roasted mahimahi with lobster tempura miso soy, free-range chicken with tamarind stuffing, veal tenderloin with caramelized endive, and duck with five-spice consommé. All dishes are explained table-side. His nightly "surprise" tasting menu is a five-course adventure for the whole table; wine pairings can be added for an additional cost. The chef doesn't make substitutions or alterations to his creations, so make sure you have no allergies or aversions to what you've ordered. The food is outstanding, but service can be a little sluggish. ⚠ **Vegetarians beware: There are few appetizers but no main courses without meat or fish.** ⑤ *Average main: $30* ⊠ *The Beach House Turks and Caicos, Lower Bight Rd. 218, The Bight* ☎ *649/946–5800* ⚓ *Reservations essential.*

**$** ✕ **Middle Caicos Cafe.** *Caribbean.* Bringing true local flavor walking distance from the main hub, try to meet Lisa the owner, as she has stories to tell, giving the food even more flavor. Lisa came over from Middle Caicos to work at "Shut Up and Drink" liquor store and started making breakfast for her favorite customers. One customer loved her cooking so much he encouraged Lisa to open her own restaurant. With true island cooking and fresh ingredients, the menu changes daily on the board, including fish, chicken, and "something else." The best local food on the island includes baked chicken, steamed fish, peas and rice, okra, and fried plantains. Customers favorites are grouper sautéed with peppers and onions and her "special seasoning." Conch stew is the island soul food. On Wednesday everything on the menu is $10. ⑤ *Average main: $12* ⊠ *Cultural Market, Lower Bight Rd., The Bight* ☎ *649/946–5435* ▭ *No credit cards* ⊙ *Closed Sun. No dinner Sat.–Thurs.*

$$ ✕**Somewhere on the Beach Café and Lounge.** *Mexican.* The Tex-Mex breakfasts here are enhanced by great views. Try the breakfast burrito, a light tortilla filled with scrambled eggs, peppers, and homemade salsa, best enjoyed while overlooking thatched umbrellas and snorkelers on the reef. For lunch, the black bean salsa and homemade guacamole score high marks. A three-tier outdoor terrace makes for terrific sunset dining, drawing a fun adult-only crowd into the evening for steak and fish with Mexican spice. The portions are always huge. There's live music many nights—Thursdays are the best. ⑤ *Average main: $18* ✉ *Coral Gardens Resort, Lower Bight Rd., The Bight* ☎ *649/941–8260* ⊕ *www.somewherecafeandlounge.com.*

$$$$ ✕**Stelle.** *Contemporary.* The setting is chic—some would even say swanky—with white fabrics blowing in the wind, diners dressed for clubbing, and tables surrounding a courtyard with views of the lighted pool. It's like a small piece of South Beach has been transported to the tropics. Even the food is chic, with such popular menu items as tortellini with black truffles, macadamia-crusted snapper with coconut rice, and charred corn and sun-dried tomato salad. On Friday and Saturday night, you may want to linger as a DJ plays music so you can dance away. ⑤ *Average main: $40* ✉ *Gansevoort Turks + Caicos, Lower Bight Rd., The Bight* ☎ *649/946–5746* ⊕ *www.gansevoorthotelgroup.com.*

## TURTLE COVE

$ ✕**Angela's Top o' the Cove New York Style Delicatessen.** *Deli.* Order deli sandwiches, salads, enticingly rich desserts, and freshly baked pastries at this island institution on Leeward Highway, just south of Turtle Cove. The location's not close to where most tourists stay, but it's worth the drive. From the deli case you can buy the fixings for a picnic; the shelves are stocked with a broad selection of fancy foodstuffs, as well as beer and wine. It's open at 6:30 am for a busy trade in coffees and cappuccinos. There's even a cheesesteak comparable to what you get in Philly. ⑤ *Average main: $9* ✉ *Leeward Hwy., Turtle Cove* ☎ *649/946–4694* ⊕ *www. provo.net/topofthecove* ⊗ *No dinner.*

$$$ ✕**Baci Ristorante.** *Italian.* Aromas redolent of the Mediterranean waft from the open kitchen as you enter this intimate eatery east of Turtle Cove. Outdoor seating is on a romantic canal-front patio, one of the lovelier settings on Provo. The menu offers a small but varied selection of Italian dishes. Veal is prominent on the menu, but main

courses also include pasta, chicken, fish, and brick-oven pizzas. You'll never see redder tomatoes than those in the tomato-and-mozzarella Caprese salad; a standout entrée is the chicken with vodka-cream sauce. House wines are personally selected by the owners and complement the well-edited wine list. Try tiramisu for dessert with a flavored coffee drink. Wear bug spray at night. ⑤ *Average main: $23* ✉ *Harbour Towne, Turtle Cove* ☎ *649/941–3044* ⊕ *baci-ristorante.com* ⊘ *Closed Sun. No lunch Sat.*

$ ✕**Greenbean.** *Café.* Although most of the fancier restaurants of Provo are terrific, sometimes you just want to pick up something fast. Start the day with breakfast sandwiches and a variety of coffee choices (Starbucks brand is brewed here). Daily specials, great paninis, and the chance to make your own sandwiches for a picnic make this a nice break from long, lingering meals. It's also a great choice for vegetarians. There's free Wi-Fi, and the restaurant also rents snorkel gear for off the beach snorkeling nearby. ⑤ *Average main: $10* ✉ *Harbour Towne, Unit 1, Turtle Cove* ☎ *649/941–2233* ⊕ *www.greenbeantci.com* ⊘ *No dinner.*

$$$$ ✕**Magnolia Wine Bar and Restaurant.** *Eclectic.* The hands-on owners here, Gianni and Tracey Caporuscio, make success seem simple. Expect well-prepared, uncomplicated dishes from all over. You can construct an excellent meal from the outstanding appetizers, which might include spring rolls and a grilled-vegetable-and-fresh-mozzarella stack. Finish your meal with the mouthwatering molten chocolate cake. The atmosphere is romantic, the presentations are attractive, and the service is careful. It's easy to see why the Caporuscios have a loyal following. The adjoining wine bar includes a handpicked list of specialty wines, which can be ordered by the glass. The marine setting is a great place to watch the sunset. ⑤ *Average main: $35* ✉ *Miramar Resort, Lower Bight Rd., Turtle Cove* ☎ *649/941–5108* ⊕ *www.magnoliaprovo.com* ⊘ *Closed Mon. No lunch.*

$$ ✕**Sharkbites Bar & Grill.** *American.* At this local favorite, the standard fare incorporates everything from the local catch in sandwiches to nachos and beer. It's a casual place for lunch—its huge deck overlooks Turtle Cove Marina, and sometimes during the day sharks will swim around it—exciting for kids. Friday-night happy hour makes this a popular place to listen to live bands and meet locals. Try listening to Quinton Dean, who just came back from a worldwide tour with Prince. Don't forget to get the best souvenir T-shirt on island. ⑤ *Average main: $17* ✉ *Turtle*

*Cove Marina, Bridge Rd., Turtle Cove* ☎649/941–5090 ⊕*www.thesharkbite.com* ⌂*Reservations not accepted.*

**$$$** ✕**Tiki Hut.** *American.* From a location overlooking the
FAMILY   marina, the ever-popular Tiki Hut serves consistently tasty, value-priced meals in a fun atmosphere. Locals take advantage of the Wednesday-night chicken-and-rib special, and the lively bar is a good place to sample local Turks Head brew. There's a special family-style menu (the best kids' menu in Provo) and kids' seating. Don't miss pizzas made with the signature white sauce, or the jerk wings, coated in a secret barbecue sauce and then grilled—they're out of this world. The restaurant can be busy, with long waits for a table, and you can reserve only with five people or more. ⑤*Average main: $20* ⊠*Turtle Cove Marina, Suzy Turn, Turtle Cove* ☎649/941–5341 ⊕*tikihut.tc.*

## LEEWARD

**$** ✕**Fresh Bakery & Bistro.** *Bakery.* A stop by this popular bakery and café makes it easy for you to pack a picnic and explore the island. You can buy salads and deli sandwiches made with bread baked daily. Specials usually include ham-and-cheese panini's and spicy chicken with grilled vegetables, all packed to go. Don't forget to end with dessert; the European-style pastries are delectable. You can even call ahead, so you can spend more time on the beach and less time waiting, but the bakery closes fairly early (at 7 pm most nights, 6:30 pm on Sunday). This is also a great place to order a special cake for a wedding, birthday, or other celebration. ⑤*Average main: $9* ⊠*The Atrium Resort, Governor's Rd., Leeward* ☎649/345–4745 ⊕*www.freshprovo. com* ⊘*No dinner.*

## DOWNTOWN

**$** ✕**Hole in the Wall.** *Caribbean.* It's mostly locals at this accurately named restaurant. The menu is heavy on the fresh catch of the day, but the restaurant also offers visitors the opportunity to get a taste of local cuisine such as oxtail and curried goat. A typical Caribbean breakfast here consists of saltfish or liver and onions with grits. Chicken, ribs, and pork chops are also on the menu. It's open late every day except for Sunday, when it closes at 3. ⑤*Average main: $11* ⊠*Williams Plaza, Old Airport Rd., Downtown* ☎649/941–4136 ⌂*Reservations not accepted* ▭*No credit cards* ⊘*No dinner Sun.*

## DISCOVERY BAY

$ ✕ **Corner Café.** *Deli.* This is the perfect stop for a quick break-fast, lunch, or early light dinner, and its location next to the supermarket makes it a convenient stop as well. Owned and operated by the IGA, the café serves very fresh food. There is a sandwich on the menu to suit almost any taste, with honey ham, prosciutto, chicken salad, and salmon among the choices. Each is made to order with bread that's baked fresh daily. This is also a great choice for your caffeine rush, with coffee, cappuccino, and espresso all available. Get your order to go if you want to have a picnic at beautiful Taylor Bay. $ *Average main: $9 ⊠ Leeward Hwy., next to Graceway IGA, Discovery Bay* ☎ *649/941–8724* ⊟ *No credit cards* ⊘ *Closed Sun.*

## BLUE HILLS

$$ ✕ **Da Conch Shack.** *Caribbean.* An institution in Provo for many years, this brightly colored beach shack is justifiably famous for its conch and seafood. The conch is fished fresh out of the shallows and broiled, spiced, cracked, or fried to absolute perfection. This is the freshest conch anywhere on the island, as the staff dive for it only after you've placed your order, but if you don't like seafood, there's also chicken. Go on a Tuesday night, when jerk chicken, peas and rice, and slaw are only $10.99, or a Thursday night when there's live music on the sand. $ *Average main: $15 ⊠ Blue Hills Rd., Blue Hills* ☎ *649/946–8877* ⊕ *www. conchshack.tc* ⊟ *No credit cards.*

$$ ✕ **Horse-Eye Jacks Beach Bar and Grill.** *American.* This little restaurant is both amazingly casual but also simply amaz-ing, sitting atop a wooden deck right on the beach in Blue Hills. A real beach bar, this local favorite serves great jerk chicken pork or ribs, burgers, and nachos. It's also locally famous for "broasted" chicken, a pressure-frying process with lower calories and carbs than traditional fried chicken. The deck can get energetic at times with live music, and during the day a spontaneous beach volleyball tournament can start on the sand. During full moons the beach barbecue party can get crowded. $ *Average main: $14 ⊠ Blue Hills Rd., Blue Hills* ☎ *649/339–1100* ⊕ *www. horseeyejacks.com.*

$$ ✕ **Three Mary Queens.** *Caribbean.* Three generations have run the popular "locals" eatery—making it the oldest res-taurant on the island—long before there was ever a hotel or resort on Provo. Ms. Martha will tell you what's on

the menu every day; always count on grouper and conch. There's always a game of Slammin' Dominoes going on, but what's best is the local gossip. Find out what's going on both sides of the political table. This is the home of the annual Conch Festival held in November. ⑤ *Average main: $18* ✉ *Millennium Hwy., Blue Hills* ☎ *649/941–5984.*

## FIVE CAYS

**$$**   ✕**Bugaloo's.** *Caribbean.* Bugaloo's beach shack started the conch craze. Bugaloo started out in Blue Hills, moved to Freeport, came back, and recently opened at a new location on the beach at Five Cays. Island attitude, with sayings such as, "Ain't saying it had to been" and "R" rated (or maybe "X") music abound. Of course, you can get conch here prepared in many different ways, as fritters, cracked, salad, and so on. There's also fresh fish and fried chicken. On Sunday afternoon there's a "conch crawl" with live music, when rum punch flows a little freer than normal and things can get lively. ⑤ *Average main: $14* ✉ *Five Cays Beach, Five Cays* ☎ *649/941–3863.*

## CHALK SOUND

**$$$**   ✕**Las Brisas Restaurant & Bar.** *Spanish.* With exquisite views
FAMILY   of Chalk Sound, the setting here is perfect. The outdoor deck and gazebo offer picture-postcard views of the neon-turquoise water of the sound. The only Spanish restaurant on Provo serves an excellent paella (if you order this, give it time—the flavors have to simmer). The menu also includes tapas, so you can nibble for lunch while you gaze at the gorgeous water. Dinner takes a little longer, as everything is made to order; you pick out your fish or meat, decide how you want it prepared, and choose a sauce for it. The views alone are worth a visit, and children are allowed to use the pool while you eat, so everybody's happy. ⑤ *Average main: $25* ✉ *Neptune Villas, Chalk Sound Rd., Chalk Sound* ☎ *649/946–5306* ⊕ *neptunevillastci.com.*

## NORTHWEST POINT

**$$$$**   ✕**The Restaurant at Amanyara.** *Eclectic.* While this restaurant doesn't have an official name, that small omission shouldn't keep you from dining here. The setting, around pavilions with pools, is unique on Provo. Some tables are by the beach to get ocean breezes, others are indoors, with air-conditioning. Bring bug spray at dusk if you're eating outside—you are surrounded by water. For guests of the resort, the restaurant is the only choice for dinner, unless you take a long and expensive taxi ride to other restaurants. If you are not an Amanyara guest, make reservations at least two days in advance for either lunch or dinner. The food is fantastic, with the freshest seafood and choicest cuts of meat available in Provo. The menu changes daily but always includes a choice of fish, meat, chicken, or lamb. The sauces have an Asian influence, with soy-infused wine reduction on the steaks and vegetable-fried rice for a side. Meat lovers will find one of the best steaks on the island here. ⑤ *Average main: $40* ⊠ *Amanyara Resort, Malcom's Road Beach, Northwest Point* ☎ *649/941–8133* ⌕ *Reservations essential.*

## WHERE TO STAY

It's rare to find a truly bad place to stay on Providenciales. Most of the hotels, resorts, and villas on Provo are impeccably maintained; all are clean and comfortable, and most offer up-to-date, modern conveniences such as air-conditioning, satellite TV, and Wi-Fi. Because Provo is relatively new to the tourism business, most resorts are just a few years old. The majority of accommodations are individually owned condos placed in a rental pool and treated as a resort. You get the best of both worlds in these condo resorts: luxurious, full living areas that come with resort amenities such as toiletries, excursion desks, and towels for the beach. Except for the Comfort Suites, Club Med, and Beaches resorts, you won't find any chains represented. Even the island's more basic accommodations are nice, with comfortable rooms with all the expected conveniences. More upscale accommodations offer pure luxury; most have full kitchens, state-of-the-art appliances, and lavish furnishings—some are probably nicer than the house you live in. The resorts offer various levels of services and run the gamut from straightforward condo complexes without restaurants or excursion desks to full-service resorts with room service and pampering on the beach. Almost all the hotels and resorts are located in the Grace Bay area, sometimes referred as Provo's "Golden Mile"; there are only a few hotels located in Turtle Cove, Northwest Point, and Chalk Sound.

Provo is one of the better islands in the Caribbean for renting a private villa; there is a plethora to choose from that offer a clean, comfortable home away from home. Villas are scattered across the island, so you can choose whether you want to be close to activity or have peace and quiet. Villas range from romantic one-bedroom homes on the beach to fantastic multi-bedroom mansions on private stretches of sand, with everything in between. If you do stay in a villa, then you'll need to rent a car, sometimes just to get to the beach. Most villas are in areas that are not close to restaurants. Some can be found in residential neighborhoods, such as Leeward, where homes may be on a canal or a couple of blocks from the beach. Several villas are in quiet Turtle Tail, behind the Graceway IGA supermarket. These villas offer views of the stunning Caicos Banks. The villas around Sapodilla Bay, Taylor Bay, and Chalk Sound usually have gorgeous views in all directions. A villa can offer a more budget-friendly vacation if you split the costs with other couples or families.

## RENTAL AGENTS

**Coldwell Banker TCI.** The agents at Coldwell Banker list some of the most beautiful vacation homes in Provo. ☏ 649/946–4969 ⊕ www.coldwellbankertci.com.

**Prestigious Properties.** Modest to magnificent condos and houses in the Leeward, Grace Bay, and Turtle Cove areas of Providenciales are available from this company. ☏ 649/946–5355 ⊕ www.prestigiousproperties.com.

**T.C. Safari.** This company manages numerous properties around Provo. ☏ 649/941–5043, 828/625–9992 ⊕ www.tcsafari.tc.

**TC Villas.** Based in Atlanta, TC Villas has hand-selected some of the most beautiful villas in Provo and has a wide selection from one-bedroom cottages to private estates. ☏ 404/467–4858 ⊕ www.TCVillas.com.

**Turks and Caicos Reservations.** Booking agents who live on island keep inventory of all the resorts and villas and are in direct contact with general managers and property managers. The company also offers rewards that include dinner vouchers or a one-day car rental, and there are extra perks for repeat bookings. They will work hard to get you the best deal, and when there are storms and delays, they can help you find emergency accommodations. ☏ 649/941–8988, 877/774–5486 ⊕ Turksandcaicosreservations.tc.

## CONCIERGE SERVICES

**After 5 Island Concierge.** Sometimes you just need help before or during your trip. After 5 Island Concierge can do everything from find you a villa rental to provide grocery delivery or arrange a talented personal chef to cook during your condo or villa stay. Virtually any service you can think of is available from this company. ☎ 649/232–3483.

Most resorts on Provo are composed of privately owned condos that are placed into the resort's rental pool when the owners are not present. Unlike at chain hotels and resorts, you cannot request a particular building, floor, or room unless you are a repeat visitor. If you fall in love with the condo, you can probably purchase it or one that's similar. There are no taxes in Turks and Caicos except for a onetime stamp-duty tax—no property tax and no rental tax—which makes owning your own piece of paradise even more tempting.

*For expanded hotel reviews, visit Fodors.com.*

## GRACE BAY

The vast majority of the hotels and resorts on Providenciales have been developed along beautiful Grace Bay, between the Turtle Cove Marina on the west and Leeward on the east.

**$$** ⊞ **The Alexandra Resort.** *Resort.* Situated on the most popular
FAMILY stretch of Grace Bay Beach, the Alexandra is within walking distance of shops, Coral Garden's snorkeling, and excellent restaurants. **Pros:** luxury for (somewhat) less, with lots of good amenities. **Cons:** some rooms have only queen beds, not kings. ⑤ *Rooms from: $325* ✉ *Princess Dr., Grace Bay* ☎ *649/946–5807, 800/704–9424* ⊕ *www.alexandraresort. com* ⇆ *88 rooms* ⊠ *No meals.*

★ **Fodor'sChoice** ⊞ **Beaches Turks & Caicos Resort Villages & Spa.**
**$$$$** *All-Inclusive. Resort.* The largest resort in the Turks and
FAMILY Caicos Islands can satisfy families who might be just as eager to spend some time apart as together, and a major renovation and expansion in Fall 2013 has made it even better. **Pros:** great place for families; all-inclusive; gorgeous pools; kids love this place. **Cons:** with an all-inclusive plan you miss out on the island's other great restaurants; excursions such as catamaran trip can get crowded; very expensive. ⑤ *Rooms from: $884* ✉ *Lower Bight Rd., Grace Bay* ☎ *649/946–8000, 800/726–3257* ⊕ *www.beaches.com* ⇆ *359 rooms, 103 suites* ⊠ *All-inclusive.*

**\$\$** ☷**Blue Water White Sands Resort.** *Rental.* This newly reno-
vated resort is in the middle of the hub, offering easy access
to nearby shops and restaurants, and is within walking distance of several different access points to Grace Bay Beach.
**Pros:** very economical rates for Provo; great management
team with strong track record; close to nightlife so no driving back. **Cons:** with everything so convenient you might
not venture out to other great places on island. ⑤*Rooms
from: \$249* ✉*382 Grace Bay Rd., Grace Bay* ☎*649/432–
8633* ⊕*www.bwwsresorts.com* ➵*10 suites* ⦿*No meals.*

**\$** ☷**Caribbean Paradise Inn.** *B&B/Inn.* Inland and about a
10-minute walk from Grace Bay Beach, this two-story bed-
and-breakfast has terra-cotta walls and cobalt-blue trim-
mings. **Pros:** pay a lot less by staying a block from the beach.
**Cons:** front desk not always manned; breakfast is extra.
⑤*Rooms from: \$145* ✉*Grace Bay* ☎*649/946–5020* ⊕*www.
caribbeanparadiseinn.com* ➵*18 rooms* ⦿*Multiple meal plans.*

**\$\$\$\$** ☷**Club Med Turkoise.** *All-Inclusive. Resort.* In contrast to
the other, more tranquil Grace Bay resorts, this energetic
property has a vibrant party atmosphere, nightly enter-
tainment, and even a flying trapeze—it caters mainly to
fun-loving singles and couples. **Pros:** all-inclusive; active;
good value; adults only (of all ages, not just young); numerous languages spoken. **Cons:** even with some renovations,
the rooms are dormlike and need updates and TLC; food
just so-so. ⑤*Rooms from: \$554* ✉*Grace Bay Rd., Grace
Bay* ☎*649/946–5500, 888/932–2582* ⊕*www.clubmed.com*
➵*293 rooms* ⦿*All-inclusive.*

**\$\$\$\$** ☷**Grace Bay Club.** *Resort.* This stylish resort retains a loyal
FAMILY following because of its helpful, attentive staff and unpretentious elegance. **Pros:** gorgeous pool and restaurant
lounge areas with outdoor couches, daybeds, and fire pits;
all guests receive a cell phone to use on the island. **Cons:**
no children allowed at Anacaona restaurant; have to stay
in Estates section to get to its pool; expensive. ⑤*Rooms
from: \$995* ✉*Grace Bay Rd., behind Grace Bay Ct., Grace
Bay* ☎*649/946–5050, 800/946–5757* ⊕*www.gracebayclub.
com* ➵*59 suites* ⦿*Breakfast.*

**\$** ☷**Grace Bay Suites.** *Hotel.* A bargain compared to most
hotels in the Grace Bay area, this hotel gives you your
money's worth, with the beach an easy one-block walk.
**Pros:** you're only a block from the beach; some luxury for
less money. **Cons:** no views; not directly on the beach; no
stove in kitchenette. ⑤*Rooms from: \$145* ✉*Grace Bay
Rd., Grace Bay* ☎*649/941–7447* ⊕*www.gracebaysuites.
com* ➵*18 studios, 6 1 bedrooms* ⦿*No meals.*

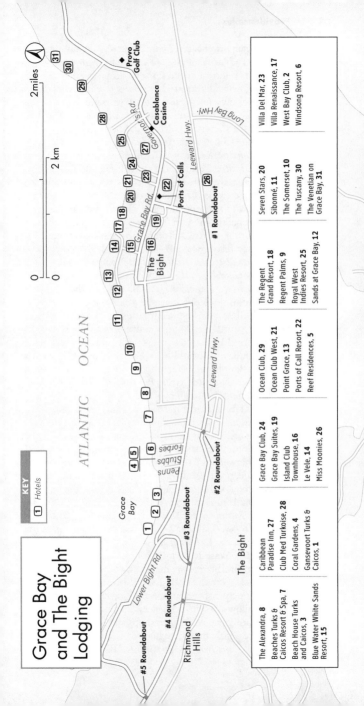

# Grace Bay and The Bight Lodging

ATLANTIC OCEAN

Grace Bay

The Bight

Richmond Hills

Provo Golf Club

Casablanca Casino

Ports of Calls

#1 Roundabout
#2 Roundabout
#3 Roundabout
#4 Roundabout
#5 Roundabout

Penns Stubbs Forbes

Lower Bight Rd.
Grace Bay Rd.
Leeward Hwy.
Governor's Rd.
Long Bay Hwy.

KEY
1 Hotels

2 miles
2 km

The Alexandra, **8**
Beaches Turks & Caicos Resort & Spa, **7**
Beach House Turks and Caicos, **3**
Blue Water White Sands Resort, **15**

Caribbean Paradise Inn, **27**
Club Med Turkoise, **28**
Coral Gardens, **4**
Gansevoort Turks & Caicos, **1**

Grace Bay Club, **24**
Grace Bay Suites, **19**
Island Club Townhouse, **16**
Le Vele, **14**
Miss Moonies, **26**

Ocean Club, **29**
Ocean Club West, **21**
Point Grace, **13**
Ports of Call Resort, **22**
Reef Residences, **5**

The Regent Grand Resort, **18**
Regent Palms, **9**
Royal West Indies Resort, **25**
Sands at Grace Bay, **12**

Seven Stars, **20**
Sibonné, **11**
The Somerset, **10**
The Tuscany, **30**
The Venetian on Grace Bay, **31**

Villa Del Mar, **23**
Villa Renaissance, **17**
West Bay Club, **2**
Windsong Resort, **6**

**$**   ⌂ **Island Club Townhouses.** *Rental.* If you're on a budget you won't find a place that gives you more for your money than this small condo complex. **Pros:** you can't get a better deal in Provo; centrally located so you can walk everywhere. **Cons:** the few condos for short-term rental go fast; no phones in the room; a block from the beach. ⑤ *Rooms from: $240* ✉ *Grace Bay Rd., Grace Bay* ☎ *649/946–5866, 877/211–3133* ⊕ *www.islandclubgracebay.com* ⇆ *12 2-bedroom apartments* ⊠ *No meals.*

**$$$**   ⌂ **Le Vele.** *Hotel.* Modern and chic, this condo resort looks as if it were transported directly from Miami's South Beach, minus the crowds. **Pros:** great central location; spacious rooms maximize the ocean views. **Cons:** residential feel isn't for everyone; the modern buildings don't blend with other resorts on the beach. ⑤ *Rooms from: $474* ✉ *Grace Bay Rd., Grace Bay* ☎ *649/941–8800, 888/272-4406* ⊕ *www. levele.tc* ⇆ *12 suites, 10 studios* ⊠ *Breakfast.*

**$$**   ⌂ **Miss Moonies.** *Rental.* A new concept for Provo, Miss Moonie proves you can have it all at a rock-bottom budget, including gorgeous apartments, a 24-hour convenience store, all-night deli, and lushly landscaped pool. **Pros:** surprisingly affordable; 24 hour convenience store is one of a kind in TCI; Marcia is a friendly host. **Cons:** concert nights can get loud (call ahead for a schedule); no website yet for easy access; only email and phone contact. ⑤ *Rooms from: $150* ✉ *Grace Bay Rd., Grace Bay* ☎ *649/941–6664* ✎ *Melicia_Fredericks@hotmail.com* ⇆ *8 condos* ⊠ *Breakfast.*

**$$$**   ⌂ **Ocean Club.** *Resort.* Enormous, locally painted pictures
FAMILY   of hibiscus make a striking first impression as you enter the reception area at one of the island's most well-established condominium resorts. **Pros:** family-friendly resort with shuttles between the two shared properties; screened balconies and porches allow a respite from incessant air-conditioning. **Cons:** although clean, furniture is dated; if no car rental, you have to take the shuttle to get closer to the "hub." ⑤ *Rooms from: $309* ✉ *Grace Bay Rd., Grace Bay* ☎ *649/946–5880, 800/457–8787* ⊕ *www.oceanclubresorts. com* ⇆ *86 suites* ⊠ *No meals.*

**$$$**   ⌂ **Ocean Club West.** *Resort.* It's central location and affordable, comfortable rooms makes this resort popular with vacationers. **Pros:** family-friendly resort with shuttles between the two shared properties; screened balconies and porches allow a respite from incessant air-conditioning; central location eases walking to shops and restaurants. **Cons:** rooms are a little bit dated; higher price point than Ocean Club. ⑤ *Rooms from: $329* ✉ *Grace Bay Rd., Grace Bay*

☎ 649/946–5880 ⊕ *oceanclubresorts.com/ocean-club-west-resort/* ⤳ *88 suites* ⊗ *Seasonal closing in Oct.* ⃟◉ *No meals.*

**$$$$** ⊞ **Point Grace.** *Resort.* Asian-influenced rooftop domes blend with Romanesque stone pillars and wide stairways in this plush resort, which offers spacious beachfront suites and romantic cottages surrounding the centerpiece: a turquoise infinity pool with perfect views of the beach. **Pros:** relaxing environment; beautiful pool. **Cons:** can be extremely quiet (there are signs reminding you around the pool). ⑤ *Rooms from: $656* ⊠ *Grace Bay Rd., Grace Bay* ☎ 649/946–5096, 888/924–7223 ⊕ *www.pointgrace.com* ⤳ *23 suites, 9 cottage suites, 2 villas* ⊗ *Closed Sept.* ⃟◉ *Breakfast.*

**$$** ⊞ **Ports of Call Resort.** *Hotel.* At the former Comfort Suites, which has been completely refurbished, vamped up, and rebranded by new management, a location a block from the beach means serious savings for those who are willing to be more than a few steps away from Grace Bay. **Pros:** economical alternative to beachfront properties; walking distance to main hub; "attached" to shopping area with restaurants. **Cons:** room key must be inserted for electricity to work (no leaving lights on when leaving); peak season standard rooms require two-night minimum (though more expensive deluxe rooms do not). ⑤ *Rooms from: $159* ⊠ *11 Sandcastle Rd., behind Port of Call, Grace Bay* ☎ 649/946–8888 ⊕ *www.portsofcallresort.com* ⤳ *98 suites* ⃟◉ *Breakfast.*

**$$$$** ⊞ **The Regent Grand Resort.** *Resort.* Even bigger and more luxurious than its sister property, Villa Renaissance, the Regent Grand is centered on a courtyard with a four-leaf-clover-shape pool that allows guests to get peace and quiet in a gorgeous setting. **Pros:** majestic architecture with huge columns and arches; central location in walking distance of numerous restaurants and shops; upscale Regent Village shops nearby. **Cons:** no restaurant here, although many options are nearby. ⑤ *Rooms from: $835* ⊠ *Regent St., Grace Bay* ☎ 649/941–7770, 877/288–3206 ⊕ *www. TheRegentGrandResort.com* ⤳ *21 suites* ⃟◉ *Breakfast.*

**$$$$** ⊞ **Regent Palms.** *Resort.* High on luxury and glitz, this is a FAMILY place where glamour meets the beach. **Pros:** great people-watching; lively; one of the best spas in the Caribbean; lots of other amenities. **Cons:** in the summer, the pool bar can get hot in the sunken area; kind of formal around the pool; sky-high rates. ⑤ *Rooms from: $1,250* ⊠ *Princess Dr., Grace Bay* ☎ 649/946–8666, 866/630–5890 ⊕ *www. regenthotels.com* ⤳ *72 suites* ⃟◉ *Breakfast.*

**$$**   ⊤**Royal West Indies Resort.** *Resort.* With a contemporary take on colonial architecture and the outdoor feel of a botanical garden, this unpretentious resort on Grace Bay Beach has plenty of garden-view and beachfront studios and suites for moderate self-catering budgets. **Pros:** the best bang for the buck on Provo; on one of the widest stretches of Grace Bay Beach. **Cons:** Club Med next door can be noisy. ⑤ *Rooms from: $310* ⊠ *Bonaventure Crescent, Grace Bay* ☎ *649/946–5004, 800/332–4203* ⊕ *www.royalwestindies. com* ⇨ *99 suites* ⦿ *No meals.*

**$$**   ⊤**Sands at Grace Bay.** *Resort.* Spacious gardens and winding
FAMILY   pools set the tone for one of Provo's most popular family resorts. **Pros:** one of the best places for families; central to shops and numerous restaurants; screened balconies and porches give an escape from incessant air-conditioning. **Cons:** the pool deck is dark wood, so keep your sandals or flip-flops handy; avoid courtyard rooms, which are not worth the price. ⑤ *Rooms from: $360* ⊠ *Grace Bay Rd., Grace Bay* ☎ *649/941–5199, 877/777–2637* ⊕ *www. thesandstc.com* ⇨ *118 suites* ⦿ *No meals.*

★ **Fodor's**Choice ⊤ **Seven Stars.** *Resort.* Fronting gorgeous Grace
**$$$$**   Bay Beach, the tallest property on the island also sets a high
FAMILY   mark for luxury with several buildings, an enormous heated pool, and huge in-room bathrooms—just about everything at Seven Stars is bigger and better than its competitors. **Pros:** beachside location; gorgeous inside and out; walking distance to everything in Grace Bay; terrific deck bar by the beach. **Cons:** some find the giant scale of the resort too big for the rest of the island. ⑤ *Rooms from: $618* ⊠ *Grace Bay Rd., Grace Bay* ☎ *649/941–3777, 866/570–7777* ⊕ *www. sevenstarsgracebay.com* ⇨ *107 suites* ⦿ *Breakfast.*

**$**   ⊤ **Sibonné Beach Hotel.** *Hotel.* Dwarfed by most of the nearby resorts, the smallest hotel on Grace Bay Beach has snug (by Provo's spacious standards) but pleasant rooms with Bermuda-style balconies and a tiny circular pool that's hardly used because the property is right on the beach. **Pros:** closest property to the beach; the island's best bargain directly on the beach. **Cons:** pool is small and dated. ⑤ *Rooms from: $175* ⊠ *Princess Dr., Grace Bay* ☎ *649/946–5547, 800/528–1905* ⊕ *www.sibonne.com* ⇨ *29 rooms, 1 apartment* ⦿ *No meals.*

**$$$$**   ⊤ **The Somerset.** *Resort.* This luxury resort has the "wow" factor, starting with the architecture and ending in your luxuriously appointed suite. **Pros:** the most beautiful architecture on Provo; located in middle, so you can still walk to snorkel, still walk to shops. **Cons:** the cheapest lock-out rooms are not worth the cost—they can get noisy; service

## Crazy for Conch

Belongers, who are descended from the first slaves from Africa and Bermuda that settled the islands in the 1600s, know that the most important thing on their islands is also their biggest export: conch. They take full advantage of every part of the conch, from shell to meat. Every restaurant in the Turks and Caicos serves some type of conch, either in a sandwich, salad, fritter, soup, or even sushi. So loved is the conch that now it's used for other things, too. Shells are sold to tourists, who may bring back two shells per person. The pink part of the shell is used for homemade jewelry, especially bracelets and earrings. Shells are crushed and used at the Regent Palms Spa

to exfoliate your skin.

Diving for conch has been incorporated into day trips. A local called Conch Man carves the shells into shapes like palm trees and other tropical objects. You can buy his creations in the Silver Deep boutique. Conch is embedded on the ledges of walls built around homes in Salt Cay, not only for a tropical look but also to keep cows and donkeys out of the yard.

The Conch Farm is the only commercial conch farm in the world, and a visit will show you how conch is grown and give you information about its many uses. You'll meet Sally and Jerry, two resident conchs who come out on cue.

---

has suffered during management changes. ⑤ *Rooms from: $950* ⊠ *Princess Dr., Grace Bay* ☎ *649/946–5900, 877/887–5722* ⊕ *www.thesomerset.com* ⟿ *53 suites* ⎮⊚⎮ *Breakfast.*

**$$$$**   ⬚ **The Tuscany.** *Resort.* This self-catering, quiet, upscale resort is the place for independent travelers to unwind around one of the prettiest pools on Provo. **Pros:** luxurious; all condos have ocean views; beautiful pool. **Cons:** no restaurant, and it's at the far end of the hub; very expensive for a self-catering resort. ⑤ *Rooms from: $950* ⊠ *Grace Bay Rd., Grace Bay* ☎ *649/941–4667, 866/359–6466* ⊕ *www. thetuscanyresort.com* ⟿ *30 condos* ⎮⊚⎮ *No meals.*

**$$$$**   ⬚ **The Venetian on Grace Bay.** *Rental.* Although it's on a quieter stretch of beach, this small luxury property offers magnificent views just minutes from the hub and across from the island's only golf course. **Pros:** brand-new property, gorgeous views from the oversize windows. **Cons:** need a car for transportation to the best restaurants and shops; no restaurant on-site. ⑤ *Rooms from: $975* ⊠ *Grace Bay Rd., Grace Bay* ☎ *649/941–3512* ☎ *866/242–0969* ⊕ *www. thevenetiangracebay.com* ⟿ *15 condos* ⎮⊚⎮ *No meals.*

**$$** ⛫ **Villa Del Mar.** *Hotel.* This resort, which opened in 2008, offers some tremendous features for the price, even though it is not directly on Grace Bay Beach. **Pros:** close to the best restaurants on the island; within walking distance of Casablanca Casino; a bargain for the luxury. **Cons:** no on-site restaurant; no views from most floors; not directly on the beach. Ⓢ *Rooms from: $350* ⊠ *Bonaventure Crescent, Grace Bay* ☎ *649/941–5160* ⊕ *www.yourvilladelmar.com* ⤵ *18 rooms, 24 suites* �ⓞⓘ *Breakfast.*

**$$$$** ⛫ **Villa Renaissance.** *Rental.* Modeled after a Tuscan villa, this luxury property is self-catering and not really a full-service resort; nevertheless, you do get daily maid service, afternoon tea or coffee at the Pavilion Bar, and a weekly manager's cocktail reception. **Pros:** luxury for less; one of the prettiest courtyards in Provo. **Cons:** the pool bar is not consistently manned; not a full-service resort. Ⓢ *Rooms from: $760* ⊠ *Ventura Dr., Grace Bay* ☎ *649/941–5300, 877/285–8764* ⊕ *www.villarenaissance.com* ⤵ *20 suites* ⓞⓘ *No meals.*

---

## THE BIGHT

**$$$** ⛫ **Coral Gardens.** *Rental.* Some of the best off-the-beach snorkeling makes this resort and its large condo units hard to resist; the best reef is the backyard. **Pros:** resort fronts one of the best off-the-beach snorkeling spots on Provo; spacious rooms all have ocean views. **Cons:** restaurant can get lively at night; car rental recommended to get to the best restaurants and shops on island; confusing management setup. Ⓢ *Rooms from: $259* ⊠ *Penn's Rd., The Bight* ☎ *649/941–5497 Coral Gardens on Grace Bay, 877/746–7800, 649/941–3713* ⊕ *www.CoralGardensonGraceBay.com* ⤵ *54 suites* ⓞⓘ *No meals.*

**$$$$** ⛫ **Gansevoort Turks + Caicos.** *Resort.* South Beach Miami chic meets island time at this gorgeous resort with modern, comfortable furnishings. **Pros:** service is pleasant and eager to please; gorgeous heated pool and beautiful rooms; great ambience. **Cons:** since this is one of Provo's few nightlife venues, Friday and Saturday nights can get a little lively; need transportation for shops and exploring. Ⓢ *Rooms from: $750* ⊠ *Lower Bight Rd., The Bight* ☎ *649/941–7555* ⊕ *www.gansevoortturksandcaicos.com* ⤵ *55 rooms, 32 suites, 4 penthouses* ⓞⓘ *Breakfast.*

**$$$** ⛫ **Reef Residences.** *Rental.* Staying in a location that is not directly on Grace Bay Beach does not mean you must sacrifice luxury, and access to some of the best off-the-beach snorkeling is a huge bonus. **Pros:** nice pool; spacious rooms; close to a great snorkel reef. **Cons:** you have to walk through another resort to get to the beach; rental car highly recommended to get around. ⑤ *Rooms from: $289* ✉ *Stubbs Rd., The Bight* ☎ 649/941–3713, 800/532–8536 ⊕ *www.reefresidence.com* ⇌ *24 suites at Reef Residences, 8 suites at Coral Gardens* ⊙ *No meals.*

★ Fodor'sChoice ⚏ **West Bay Club.** *Resort.* One of Provo's newest
$$ resorts has a prime location on a pristine stretch of Grace Bay Beach just steps away from the best off-the-beach snorkeling. **Pros:** all rooms have a beach view; contemporary architecture makes it stand out from other resorts; amazing luxury for the price. **Cons:** you'll need transportation to go shopping and to get to the main hub. ⑤ *Rooms from: $365* ✉ *Lower Bight Rd., The Bight* ☎ 649/946–8550 ⊕ *www. thewestbayclub.com* ⇌ *46 suites* ⊙ *Breakfast.*

★ Fodor'sChoice ⚏ **Windsong Resort.** *Resort.* On a gorgeous beach
$$$ lined with several appealing resorts, Windsong stands out for two reasons: the Sail Provo program and a magnificent pool. **Pros:** the pool is the coolest; Sail Provo; gorgeous huge bathrooms. **Cons:** studios only have a refrigerator and microwave; thinner stretch of beachfront here. ⑤ *Rooms from: $390* ✉ *Stubbs Rd., Lower Bight* ☎ 649/941–7700, 800/946–3766 ⊕ *www.windsongresort.com* ⇌ *16 studios, 30 suites* ⊙ *No meals.*

## TURTLE TAIL

$$ ⚏ **Harbour Club Villas.** *Rental.* Although not on the beach, this small complex of villas is by the marina, making it a good base for scuba diving and bonefishing. **Pros:** nice value; great base for divers; personable and friendly hosts. **Cons:** need a car to get around island; not close to the better beaches; accommodations are a bit rustic. ⑤ *Rooms from: $255* ✉ *36 Turtle Tail Dr., Turtle Tail* ☎ 649/941–5748, 866/456–0210 ⊕ *www.harbourclubvillas.com* ⇌ *6 villas* ⊙ *No meals.*

## TURTLE COVE

$$$ ⚏ **La Vista Azul.** *Rental.* You can save money by staying slightly away from the beach without giving up luxury or location. **Pros:** space and luxury for a fraction of the cost of Grace Bay; views from the rooms are gorgeous; free Wi-Fi. **Cons:** too many stairs (three flights up from lobby to reach the elevators); rental car or taxi needed to get to popular restaurants and sights; parking lot is at elevator level. ⑤ *Rooms from: $275* ✉ *Lower Bight Rd., Turtle Cove* ☎ 649/946–8522 ✐ *reservations@lvaresort.com* ⊕ *www. lavistaazulresorttci.com* ⇌ *23 condos.*

## CLOSE UP What Is a Potcake?

Potcakes are indigenous dogs of the Bahamas and Turks and Caicos islands. Traditionally, these strays would be fed leftovers from the bottom of the pot, hence the name. Much is being done today to control the stray-dog population. The TCSPCA and Potcake Place are two agencies working to find homes for the puppies. You can do a good deed by adopting one of these gorgeous pups; they have received all the shots and have all the paperwork required to bring them into the United States. Even if you don't adopt, you can help by volunteering to bring one back to its adopted family. Clearing customs in the United States is actually easier when you bring back a potcake! For more information on how you can help, check out the website for Potcake Place (⊕ *www.potcakeplace.com*).

**$** ⛯ **Turtle Cove Inn.** *B&B/Inn.* This pleasant two-story inn is affordable and comfortable. **Pros:** very reasonable prices for Provo; nice marina views. **Cons:** not on the beach; requires a car to get around. ⑤ *Rooms from: $99* ⊠ *Turtle Cove Marina, Turtle Cove* ☎ *649/946–4203, 800/887–0477* ⊕ *www.turtlecoveinn.com* ⤴ *28 rooms, 2 suites* ⏉ *No meals.*

## NORTHWEST POINT

**★ Fodor'sChoice** ⛯ **Amanyara.** *Resort.* If you seek seclusion,
**$$$$** peace, and tranquillity in a Zen-like atmosphere—and you're ready to pay a lot for it—this is your place. **Pros:** on one of the best beaches on Provo; resort is quiet and secluded. **Cons:** isolated; far from restaurants, excursions, and other beaches; probably the most expensive place to stay in Provo. ⑤ *Rooms from: $1,650* ⊠ *Northwest Point* ☎ *649/941–8133* ⊕ *www.amanresorts.com* ⤴ *40 pavilions* ⏉ *No meals.*

**$$** ⛯ **Northwest Point Resort.** *Resort.* Miles from anywhere, this resort should be your destination if you need complete solitude. **Pros:** landscaping is lush and well maintained; kitchens allow you to do some cooking on your own. **Cons:** on a grassy beach that's more attractive to turtles than swimmers; far from everything; restaurant only opens seasonally and has limited service. ⑤ *Rooms from: $295* ⊠ *Millennium Hwy., Northwest Point* ☎ *649/941–8961* ⊕ *www.northwestpointresort.com* ⤴ *49 rooms* ⏉ *No meals* ⤳ *3-night minimum during peak season.*

## LEEWARD

**$$** ⛄ **The Atrium.** *Rental.* A short, 10-minute walk to Grace Bay,
FAMILY this resort offers luxury, upscale furnishings, and beach
chairs and umbrellas set up on an isolated beachfront, all
for a fraction of the price as staying at the hub. **Pros:** amaz-
ing luxury for the money; beachfront setup is isolated with
no crowds; quiet neighborhood. **Cons:** rental car required
for almost everything; only queen-size beds; studios have
only kitchenettes. ⑤ *Rooms from: $179* ✉ *Governor's Rd.,
Leeward* ☎ *649/333–0101, 888/592–7885* ⊕ *www.theatri-
umresorttci.com* ⤳ *38 suites* ⫪ *No meals.*

# SPORTS AND THE OUTDOORS

## BICYCLING

Most hotels have bicycles available for guests, or you can
rent one from an independent company. Stick to the side-
walks on Grace Bay Road for safety; drivers don't pay
much attention to bikes, and you'll create less dust on this
dry island. *Big Blue Unlimited also offers biking trips (see
⇨ Tours, below).*

**Caicos Cyclery.** Beach cruisers start at $25 daily, mountain
bikes at $40 daily. Discounts apply on rentals of more than
two days. ✉ *Venture House W101, Grace Bay Rd., Grace
Bay* ☎ *649/941–7544* ⊕ *www.caicoscyclery.com.*

**Caicos Wheels.** Scooters, dune buggies, and off-road dirt
bikes are all available from Caicos Wheels. ✉ *Grace Bay
Ct., Grace Bay* ☎ *649/242–6592* ⊕ *www.caicoswheels.com.*

**Natique Sports.** This company rents beach cruisers and
mountain bikes for $25 to $40 a day, with discounts for
renting them more than three days. They are conveniently
located on Grace Bay Road next to Regent Village. ✉ *Ven-
ture House, Venture Rd., Grace Bay* ☎ *649/941–7544*
⊕ *www.nautiquesports.com.*

**Scooter Bob's.** You can rent beach cruisers at Scooter Bob's
for $15 a day. The company also offers a pickup service.
✉ *Turtle Cove Marina, Turtle Cove* ☎ *649/946–4684*
⊕ *www.provo.net/Scooter.*

## BOATING AND SAILING

Provo's calm, reef-protected seas combine with constant easterly trade winds for excellent sailing conditions. Several multihulled vessels offer charters with snorkeling stops, food and beverage service, and sunset vistas. Prices range from $39 per person for group trips (subject to passenger minimums) to $600 or more for private charters. Caicos Adventures (see ⇨ *Diving and Snorkeling, below*) also offers the *Lady K*, a 38-foot luxury cruiser that can be chartered for individualized itineraries. Big Blue Unlimited (*see* ⇨ *Tours, below*) also offers boat charters.

FAMILY **Beluga Sailboat.** Beluga Sailboat offers private charters for six to eight passengers through the cays. Captain Tim knows these waters: he's been sailing for more than two decades. This is true sailing, no motors allowed. Tim will pick you up and take you to the marina where his boat is moored. ☎ *649/946–4396* ⊕ *www.sailbeluga.com.*

★ **Fodor'sChoice Caicos Dream Tours.** Caicos Dream Tours offers several snorkeling trips, including one that has you diving for conch before lunch on a gorgeous beach. The company also offers private charters. ⊠ *Alexandra Resort, Princess Dr., Grace Bay* ☎ *649/231–7274* ⊕ *www.caicosdreamtours.com.*

★ **Fodor'sChoice Island Vibes.** Shaun Dean makes these excursions
FAMILY stand out, since he grew up on these waters. If conditions are right, he'll have you snorkel the "abyss," where the reef drops 6,000 feet. The sight is amazing. His boat is also the best on Provo, with a diving board on the roof as well as a bathroom. ⊠ *Turtle Cove Marina, Turtle Cove* ☎ *649/231–8423* ⊕ *www.islandvibestours.com.*

**Kenard Cruises.** This luxury private catamaran is first-class all the way, including a chef who can prepare gourmet meals, a 42-inch TV, air-conditioning, and Bose surround sound. It can be chartered for a half day or full day on a custom itinerary, so you can feel like a celebrity. ☎ *649/232–3866* ⊕ *www.kenardcruises.com.*

**Sail Provo.** Very popular for private charters, Sail Provo also runs 52-foot and 48-foot catamarans on scheduled half-day, full-day, sunset, and kid-friendly glowworm cruises (these are held in the first few days after full moons, when underwater creatures light up the sea's surface for several days). ⊠ *Windsong Resort, Stubbs Rd., The Bight* ☎ *649/946–4783* ⊕ *www.sailprovo.com.*

**Silver Deep.** Silver Deep sailing trips include time for snorkeling and beachcombing at a secluded beach. If you're thinking of fishing, keep in mind that Captain Arthur Dean here is said to be among the Caribbean's finest bonefishing guides. ⊠ *Ocean Club West Plaza, Grace Bay Rd., Grace Bay* ☎ *649/946–5612* ⊕ *www.silverdeep.com.*

**Sun Charters.** The *Atabeyra,* operated by Sun Charters, is a retired rumrunner and the choice of residents for special events. Sunset rum punch parties and glowworm excursions are its specialty. There are also regularly scheduled sunset and half-day snorkeling cruises if you don't want to do a charter. ⊠ *Leeward Marina, Leeward* ☎ *649/941–5363* ⊕ *www.suncharters.tc.*

**Undersea Explorer.** For sightseeing below the waves, try a semi-submarine, the *Undersea Explorer,* operated by Caicos Tours out of the Turtle Cove Marina. You can stay dry within the small, lower observatory as it glides along on a one-hour tour of the reef, with large viewing windows on either side. The trip costs $55. ⊠ *Turtle Cove Marina, Turtle Cove* ☎ *649/231–0006* ⊕ *www.caicostours.com.*

**Wild One.** Thrill-seekers will enjoy this jetboat ride that combines 360-degree spins and heart-racing nose-offs in as shallow as 9 inches of water. You may get wet! The boat is operated by Caicos Tours out of Turtle Cove Marina. ⊠ *Turtle Cove Marina, Turtle Cove* ☎ *649/431–9453* ⊕ *www.caicostours.com.*

## DIVING AND SNORKELING

★ **Fodor's Choice** Scuba diving was the sport that drew visitors to the Turks and Caicos islands in the 1970s. Diving in the Turks and Caicos—especially off Grand Turk, South Caicos, and Salt Cay—is still considered among the best in the world.

Off Providenciales, dive sites are along the north shore's barrier reef. Most sites can be reached in anywhere from 10 minutes to 1½ hours. Dive sites feature spur-and-groove coral formations atop a coral-covered slope. Popular stops like **Aquarium, Pinnacles,** and **Grouper Hole** have large schools of fish, turtles, nurse sharks, and gray reef sharks. From the south side dive boats go to **French Cay, West Caicos, South West Reef,** and **Northwest Point.** Known for typically calm conditions and clear water, the West Caicos Marine National Park is a favorite stop. The area has dramatic walls and marine life, including sharks, eagle rays, and octopus, with large stands of pillar coral and huge barrel sponges.

## Giving Back

Although the Turks and Caicos Islands is an upscale destination, that doesn't mean the nation has no one in need. You can feel good not just because you've had a fantastic time on the world's most beautiful beach, but also because you have given back to others. Here are some worthwhile organizations you can contribute to.

■ **Caicos Dream Tours.** Kim, the owner, takes clothing donations to children in need on North Caicos. She also takes a boat over to North to feed them during school hours. ⊕ *caicosdreamtours.com.*

■ **Edward C Gartland Youth Centre.** This organization helps empower the youth of TCI, keeping them off the streets. ⊕ *Ecgyouthcentre.com.*

■ **Potcake Place.** This organization rescues stray puppies from around the islands. You can donate dog items that are hard to find on an island (toys, formula, etc.). You can also volunteer to be a courier to take puppies to their forever homes, or you can "adopt" one for the day to take to the beach (or forever, for that matter). ⊕ *www.potcakeplace.com.*

■ **Provo's Children's Home.** This organization takes in orphans and is always in need of some kind of contribution. Requested items can be viewed at the website ⊕ *www.pch.tc.*

■ **The TCI National Trust.** The Trust helps with preservation throughout the islands. ⊕ *Nationaltrust.tc.*

■ **Turks and Caicos Reef Fund.** Helping to improve the awareness of the reefs as well as to preserve them, the organization also has an annual raffle fund-raiser with awesome prizes that may include free nights at Parrot Cay. ⊕ *Tcreef.org.*

■ **The Turks & Caicos Rotary Club.** They give back in many ways, including eye-testing for school kids, dictionaries handed out, cleanup around the island. ⊕ *Rotary.tc.*

The reef and wall drop-offs thrive with bright, unbroken coral formations and lavish numbers of fish and marine life. Mimicking the idyllic climate, waters are warm all year, averaging 76°F to 78°F in winter and 82°F to 84°F in summer. With minimal rainfall and soil runoff, visibility is usually good and frequently superb, ranging from 60 feet to more than 150 feet. An extensive system of marine national parks and boat moorings, combined with an ecoconscious mind-set among dive operators, contributes to an uncommonly pristine underwater environment.

Dive operators in Provo regularly visit sites at **Grace Bay** and **Pine Cay** for spur-and-groove coral formations and bustling reef diving. They make the longer journey to the dramatic walls at **North West Point** and **West Caicos** depending on weather conditions. Instruction from the major diving agencies is available for all levels and certifications, even technical diving. An average one-tank dive costs $45; a two-tank dive, $90. There are also two live-aboard dive boats available for charter working out of Provo. *Island Vibes also offers snorkeling and diving trips (see ⇨ Boating and Sailing, above).*

**Big Blue Unlimited.** This ecotour operator got its start offering diving trips back when Provo was known only to divers. Today, they offer trips that concentrate solely on snorkeling (where other companies also have beach stops), so if you're snorkel-crazy this is the company to go with. They will take you out to West Caicos and even stop at the edge of the banks where walls drop to 6,000 feet and to a spot where you can snorkel over remains of an old shipwreck. The company's scuba trips take you to Northwest Point or West Caicos and French Cay. ⊠ *Leeward Marina, Marina Rd., Leeward* ☎ *649/946–5034* ⊕ *www.bigblueunlimited.com.*

**Caicos Adventures.** Run by the friendly Frenchman Fifi Kuntz, Caicos Adventures offers daily trips to West Caicos, French Cay, and Molasses Reef. The company owns several boats, including the *Lady K,* a luxury motorboat available for private charters. ⊠ *Regent Village, Grace Bay Rd., Grace Bay* ☎ *649/941–3346* ⊕ *www.tcidiving.com.*

**Dive Provo.** Dive Provo is a PADI five-star operation that runs daily one- and two-tank dives to popular Grace Bay sites as well as West Caicos. ⊠ *Ports of Call, Grace Bay Rd., Grace Bay* ☎ *649/946–5040, 800/234–7768* ⊕ *www.diveprovo.com.*

**Provo Turtle Divers.** Provo Turtle Divers, which also operates out of the Ocean Club and Ocean Club West, has been on Provo since the 1970s. The staff is friendly, knowledgeable, and unpretentious. ⊠ *Turtle Cove Marina, Turtle Cove* ☎ *649/946–4232, 800/833–1341* ⊕ *www.provoturtledivers.com.*

**Snuba Turks & Caicos.** Snuba Turks & Caicos offers the next-best thing to diving for a noncertified diver; it's completely different from snorkeling but requires no experience. With the Surface Nexus Underwater Breathing Apparatus, you go down to the reef like a scuba diver, but your air tank stays on the surface. Owner Jodi will take a picture of you down below for a keepsake. Children must be at least eight years old to participate. Using a catamaran, Snuba trips now include snorkeling and going to the better reefs of West Caicos and French Cay. The year-round location is at the marina at Coral Gardens, but during high season there's a second location in Turtle Cove Marina. ⊠ *South Side Marina, Lower Bight* ☎ *649/333–7333* ⊕ *www. snubaturksandcaicos.com.*

**Turks & Caicos Aggressor II.** The *Turks & Caicos Aggressor II,* a live-aboard dive boat, plies the islands' pristine sites with weekly charters from Turtle Cove Marina. Nine staterooms with air-conditioning, TVs, and DVD players, plus communal sundecks, wet bars, and hot tubs, keep you spoiled on the water. You're met on arrival at the Providenciales Airport and taken directly to the ship. ☎ *800/348–2628* ⊕ *www.turksandcaicosaggressor.com.*

## FISHING

The islands' fertile waters are great for angling—anything from bottom- and reef-fishing (most likely to produce plenty of bites and a large catch) to bonefishing and deep-sea fishing (among the finest in the Caribbean). Each July the Caicos Classic Catch & Release Tournament attracts anglers from across the islands and the United States who compete to catch the biggest Atlantic blue marlin, tuna, or wahoo. For any fishing activity, you are required to purchase a $15 visitor's fishing license; operators generally furnish all equipment, drinks, and snacks. Prices range from $100 to $375, depending on the length of trip and size of boat. Captain Arthur Dead of Silver Deep (*see* ⇨ *Boating and Sailing, above*) is said to be among the Caribbean's finest bonefishing guides.

**Grand Slam Fishing Charters.** For deep-sea fishing trips in search of marlin, sailfish, wahoo, tuna, barracuda, and shark, look up this company. ⊠ *Turtle Cove Marina, Turtle Cove* ☎ *649/231–4420* ⊕ *www.gsfishing.com.*

**Gwendolyn Fishing Charters.** Gwendolyn sets up deep-sea fishing trips for marlin, sailfish, wahoo, tuna, barracuda, and shark. ⊠ *Turtle Cove Marina, Turtle Cove* ☎ *649/946–5321* ⊕ *www.fishtci.com.*

## GOLF

Golfing in the Caribbean can be quite an experience. The Provo Golf Club in Provo has one of the finest layouts in the islands. Along with its smallish greens, the course is well manicured. If you forget your clubs, don't worry; you can rent a set that will accommodate your game. After a challenging round be sure to grab a drink or quick bite in the clubhouse that overlooks the 18th green. Usually, flamingos are spotted at the 5th green. Bring your "A" game, as this is truly a shot-maker's course.

**Fun World TCI.** At this amusement park, there's mini-golf and all kinds of other activities to keep families happy, including go-carts, a rock wall, and a small arcade. ⊠ *Long Bay Rd., Leeward* ☎ *649/231–4653* ⊕ *www.funworldtci.com* ⊡ *Mini-golf: $15.*

★ **Fodor'sChoice Provo Golf and Country Club.** Among the Caribbean's top courses, the 18 holes here (par 72) are a combination of lush greens and fairways, rugged limestone outcroppings, and freshwater lakes. Fees are $160 for 18 holes with shared cart. The club also rents tennis equipment for use on its two lighted courts, which are among the island's best. Nonmembers can play until 5 pm for $10 per hour (reservation required). ⊠ *Governor's Rd., Grace Bay* ☎ *649/946–5991* ⊕ *www.provogolfclub.com.*

## HELICOPTER TOURS

**TCI Helicopters.** Taking a tour on one of these comfortable helicopters is the best way to see the Blue Hole and a different view of Mudjin Harbour. ⊠ *Tropicana Plaza, Leeward Hwy., Grace Bay* ☎ *649/941–5079* ⊕ *www.tcihelicopters.tc.*

## HORSEBACK RIDING

**Provo Ponies.** Provo Ponies offers morning and afternoon rides for all levels. A 60-minute ride costs $75; a 90-minute ride is $90. Reservations are required, and there is a 200-pound weight limit. You can get a pickup at your Grace Bay hotel or villa (Grace Bay area only) for an additional $10 per person, which is a good deal if you don't have a rental car. It's closed on weekends. ⊠ *Long Bay* ☎ *649/946–5252* ⊕ *www.provoponies.com.*

## PADDLEBOARDING

Stand-up paddleboarding is one of the fastest growing sports in the Caribbean. In addition to Paddleboard Provo, some windsurfing outfitters rent the board, including Water Play Provo and Windsurfing Provo.

**Paddleboard Provo.** If you want to take part in the newest trendy sport, stand-up paddleboarding, then this is where you should head. You can rent paddleboards (delivery to villas and hotels is available) or take a paddleboarding tour through Mangrove Cay and the Leeward Channel. The company also rents kayaks. ✉ *Venture House, Grace Bay Rd., across from Yoshi's Sushi, Grace Bay* ☎ *649/431–6890, 649/941–7544* ⊕ *paddleboardprovo.com.*

## PARASAILING

**Captain Marvin's Watersports.** A 15-minute parasailing flight over Grace Bay is available for $75 (single) or $120 (tandem) from Captain Marvin's Watersports, who will pick you up at your hotel for your flight. The views as you soar over the bite-shape Grace Bay area, with spectacular views of the barrier reef, are unforgettable. ☎ *649/231–0643* ⊕ *captainmarvinswatersports.com/.*

**SkyPilot Parasail.** This company offers parasailing. You'll recognize their sails immediately as they travel up and down Grace Bay. They have the big smiley face on the sail. ☎ *649/333–3000* ⊕ *www.skypilotparasail.com.*

## TENNIS

You can rent tennis equipment at the Provo Golf and Country Club and play on the two lighted courts, which are among the island's best. Nonmembers can play until 5 pm for $10 per hour (reservation required). *See ⇨ Golf for more information.*

## TOURS

**Big Blue Unlimited.** The educational ecotours from Big Blue include three-hour kayak trips and land-focused guided journeys around the family islands. Its Coastal Ecology and Wildlife tour is a kayak adventure through red mangroves to bird habitats, rock iguana hideaways, and natural fish nurseries. The Middle Caicos Bicycle Adventure gets you on a bike to explore the island, touring limestone caves in Conch Bar with a break for lunch with the Forbes family in the village of Bambarra. Packages are $255 for adults. No children under 12 are allowed. ✉ *Leeward Marina, Marina Rd., Leeward* ☎ *649/946–5034* ⊕ *www.bigblue.tc.*

**Concha Woncha Tours.** For a different tour of the island, let the air-conditioned turquoise trolley be your guide. The tour includes Conch World, admission to the Cultural Show, souvenir picture of Chalk Sound, and a full lunch at Da Conch Shack. Tours last 3½ hours and are available on Monday, Wednesday, and Friday with a 10-person minimum. The trolley can also be chartered for special events (it would be fun for a wedding). This is not a cheap tour (the adult rate is $119), but you are picked up at your hotel or condo. ☎ *649/231–5665* ⊕ *conchawonchatours.com* ⊗ *Tours on Mon., Wed., and Fri.* ⊗ *Closed Sept.*

**Paradise Scooters.** New Vespa tours have arrived in Provo, where John and Rosie guide you on an island tour, including Conch Farm, Blue Hills, Sapadilla Bay, and Chalk Sound; lunch at Bugaloo's is included. Tours cost $99. The company also rents scooters, bicycles, and (soon) cars from their Grace Bay Plaza location, including electric scooters that last three to four hours on a charge. ✉ *Grace Bay Plaza, Grace Bay Rd., Grace Bay* ☎ *649/333–3333* ⊕ *www. paradisescooters.tc.*

## WATERSKIING

**Nautique Sports.** Nautique Sports offers a water-sports dream. What better place to learn to ski than on the calm, crystal-clear waters of Providenciales. A great company for beginners, Nautique offers private instruction and will have you skiing in no time. Experts can try barefoot skiing. The company also rents kitesurfing equipment and sells all sorts of water sports equipment and clothing. There's another office at Graceway Sportscenter on Leeward Highway behind Graceway IGA in Discovery Bay (☎ *649/231–6890*). ✉ *Ventura House West 101, Grace Bay Rd.* ☎ *649/941– 7544* ⊕ *www.nautiquesports.com.*

## WINDSURFING

Although the water appears calm, the breezes always blow along Provo's northern shore. Most resorts will provide Windsurfers. If you're on Grace Bay Beach, stay inside the white buoys; boats can pass by beyond them. Nautique Sports also rents kite-surfing equipment *(see Waterskiing, above).*

**Water Play Provo.** Right on the beach, they have windsurfing, stand-up paddleboards, and kayaks for multiple-day or weekly rentals. ⊠ *Ocean Club, Grace Bay Rd., Grace Bay* ☎ *649/231–3122* ⊕ *www.waterplayprovo.com.*

**Windsurfing Provo.** Windsurfers find the calm, turquoise water of Grace Bay ideal. Windsurfing Provo also rents kayaks, Windsurfers, Hobie Cats, and stand-up paddleboards (the latest popular craze on the island), and offers windsurfing instruction. There's another branch at Ocean Club West. ⊠ *Ocean Club, Grace Bay Rd., Grace Bay* ☎ *649/946–5649* ⊕ *www.windsurfingprovo.tc.*

# SHOPPING

Provo is not really a shopping destination, and you won't find bargains here. However, there is enough upscale shopping to keep your wallet busy, from tropical clothes and jewelry to art prints and accessories. The shopping areas continue to expand; new buildings are being added to Saltmills Plaza and Regent Village. The major resorts have small boutiques with signature items, so don't forget to check them out.

## SHOPPING AREAS

There are several main shopping areas in Provo: Grace Bay has the newer **Saltmills** complex and **La Petite Place** retail plaza, not to mention **Regent Village,** as well as the original **Ports of Call** shopping village. Two markets on the beach near the Ocean Club and the Beaches Turks & Caicos Resort & Spa allow for barefoot shopping.

Handwoven straw baskets and hats, polished conch-shell crafts, paintings, wood carvings, model sailboats, handmade dolls, and metalwork are crafts native to the islands and nearby Haiti. The natural surroundings have inspired local and international artists to paint, sculpt, print, craft, and photograph; most of their creations are on sale in Providenciales.

## SPAS

Except for Parrot Cay, Provo is the best destination in the Turks and Caicos if you are looking or a spa vacation. The spas here offer treatments with all the bells and whistles, and most get good word of mouth. Most of Provo's high-end resorts have spas, but if you're staying at a villa, Spa Tropique will even come to you.

## Local Souvenirs

What should you bring home after a fabulous vacation in the Turks and Caicos? Here are a few suggestions, some of which are free!

If you comb Pelican Beach or go on a conch-diving excursion, bring two conch shells (the maximum number allowed) home. Remember, only the shell, no living thing, is allowed. However, no conch shells may be exported during the "season" (July 15 to October 15), and this includes any bought in a gift shop.

You'll find locally made ceramics at Art Provo and at Turks & Caicos National Trust (at Town Center Mall or next to Island Scoop Ice Cream).

There are two cultural centers, one between Ocean Club and Club Med, and the other across the street from Veranda Resort entrance. Here you'll find batik clothing and locally made jewelry. Custom-made pieces can be ordered.

One of the best souvenirs is the hardcover coffee-table cookbook from the Red Cross. Not only is it gorgeous, featuring recipes from all the great chefs of the Turks and Caicos, but the proceeds help the Red Cross.

The best free souvenir—besides your phenomenal tan—is a potcake puppy. The puppy you adopt comes with carrier, papers, and all the shots—and will remind you year after year of your terrific vacation.

**Anani Spa at Grace Bay Club.** Anani Spa at Grace Bay Club is on the Villas side of the complex; the six treatment rooms have alfresco showers, but treatments can also be performed on your balcony at Grace Bay Club facing the ocean. One of the most popular treatments is the Exotic Lime and Ginger Salt Glow; not only will it polish your skin, but the aroma it leaves on your skin is worth the treatment. ⊠ *Villas at Grace Bay Club, Bonaventure Crescent, Grace Bay* ☎ *649/946–5050* ⊕ *www.gracebayclub.com.*

**Beaches Red Line Spa.** Open to nonresort guests, this spa has one hot plunge pool and one cold plunge pool to get the circulation going. During special hours, it offers kid's treatments, too. Although Beaches is an all-inclusive resort, spa treatments are an additional charge to guests. ⊠ *Beaches Turks & Caicos Resort Villages & Spa, Lower Bight Rd., Grace Bay* ☎ *649/946–8000* ⊕ *www.beaches.com.*

**Como Shambhala at Parrot Cay.** Asian holistic treatments, yoga with the world's leading teachers in a stunning pavilion, and a signature health-conscious cuisine are all part of the program here. The infinity pool, Pilates studio, steam room, sauna, and outdoor Jacuzzi make you feel complete. If you're staying in Provo, you can call for reservations, but you have to pay for the boat ride to Parrot Cay. Some consider this one of the finest spas in the world, and you'd be hard-pressed to find a better one in the Turks and Caicos. ✉ *Parrot Cay Resort, Parrot Cay* ☎ *649/946–7788* ⊕ *www. comoshambhala.com.*

**Regent Spa.** Regent Spa is so gorgeous that it has been featured on several travel magazine covers. A reflecting pool with majestic date palms sets the scene. The signature treatment, a "Mother of Pearl Body Exfoliation," uses hand-crushed local conch shells to revitalize and soften skin. On an island with several terrific spas, the combination of a beautiful setting and treatments incorporating local ingredients makes this a standout. ✉ *Regent Palms, Princess Dr., Grace Bay* ☎ *649/946–8666* ⊕ *www.regenthotels.com.*

**Spa Sanay.** Spa Sanay, an independent spa in a small shopping center on Grace Bay Road, offers treatments at 50% off for children. With a full line of services, it's a great place to have your hair and nails done for weddings. ✉ *Grace Bay Ct., Grace Bay Rd., Grace Bay* ☎ *649/946–8212.*

**Spa Tropique.** You pick the place, and this spa comes to you—an ideal option for those in more isolated villas who can't bear to leave their island paradise; the spa can also come to your hotel room (provided your hotel has no spa of its own). Have your treatment on your balcony, or on the beach or by the pool, which will make the treatment seem extra special. Spa Tropique's one-of-a-kind Turks Island Salt Glow incorporates local salts from Grand Turk and Salt Cay. The spa also has locations at Ocean Club West and The Sands Resort. ✉ *Ports of Call Shopping Center, Grace Bay Rd., Grace Bay* ☎ *649/331–2040* ⊕ *www. spatropique.com.*

**Teona Spa.** Treatments here include the "Two Hot to Handle" couples massage, which includes a warming Boreh mask and Mediterranean hot-oil massage. Afterwards you can wind down with spice tea or a glass of wine. ✉ *The Regent Grand Resort, Regent St., Grace Bay* ☎ *649/941–5051* ⊕ *www.theregentgrandresort.com.*

**Thalasso Spa at Point Grace.** Thalasso Spa at Point Grace has three whitewashed open-air cabanas on the dunes looking out to the beach. French skin oils and the latest European techniques are incorporated in all skin treatments, along with elements of the ocean, including sea mud, seaweed, and sea salt. The setting alone, with the breezes and views of Grace Bay, is worth the stop. ✉ *Point Grace Resort, Grace Bay Rd., Grace Bay* ☎ *649/946–5096* ⊕ *www.pointgrace.com.*

## GRACE BAY

### ART AND CRAFT GALLERIES

**Anna's Art Gallery and Studio.** Anna's sells original artworks, silk-screen paintings, sculptures, and handmade sea-glass jewelry. ✉ *The Saltmills, Grace Bay* ☎ *649/231–3293.*

**ArtProvo.** This is the island's largest gallery of designer wall art, but native crafts, jewelry, handblown glass, candles, and other gift items are also available. Featured artists include Trevor Morgan, from Salt Cay, and Dwight Outten. ✉ *Regent Village, Regent St., Grace Bay* ☎ *649/941–4545* ⊕ *www.artprovo.tc.*

**Making Waves Art Studio.** At this gallery, Sara the proprietor paints turquoise scenes, often on wood that doesn't require framing—they're surprisingly affordable. She also gives group art lessons at the studio. ✉ *Regent Village, Regent St., Grace Bay* ☎ *649/242–9588* ⊕ *www.makingwavesart.com.*

### CLOTHING FOR WOMEN

**Caicos Wear Boutique.** This store is filled with casual resort wear, including Caribbean-print shirts, swimsuits from Brazil, sandals, beach jewelry, and gifts. ✉ *Regent Village, Grace Bay Rd., Grace Bay* ☎ *649/941–3346.*

### FOOD

Grocery shopping in Provo is almost as good as at home, with all the American, British, and Canadian brands you crave. Because everything has to be flown in, expect to pay up to 50% more than for similar purchases in the United States. Even many hard-to-find products and special dietary foods can be found on Provo. Shipments come in on Sunday, so Monday is your best food-shopping bet.

Beer is expensive, rum is cheaper, and stores are prohibited by law from selling alcohol on Sunday. Although it's tempting to bring in your own cooler of food, remember that some airlines charge for checked bags, and there is the risk of losing luggage. More than likely, if it's allowed in the States, it's allowed in Provo—meat, fish, and vegetables can be brought in if frozen and vacuum-sealed; always ask your airline if you will be allowed to check or bring a cooler. If you're traveling for more than a week, then you may save enough money by bringing provisions here to make it worth the trouble. But if you're staying on Provo, there will be no problem buying anything you need.

There's only one 24-hour store on Providenciales, Miss Moonies (*see* ⇨ *Where to Eat*), which has a pretty good selection of prepared foods.

**FOTTAC.** At Regent Village, this food-minded gift shop (the name stands for Flavours of the Turks and Caicos) also carries local Bambarra Rum and spices and sauces made with it, Turk's Head Beer, T-shirts, wine glasses, mugs, and locally made soaps. ⊠ *Regent Village, Regent St., Grace Bay* ☎ *649/946–4536* ⊕ *www.bambarrarum.com.*

**Gourmet Goods.** Gourmet Goods caters weddings and parties, with spring rolls, smoked salmon, wings and chicken satay trays, prepared foods such as meat loaf and lasagna, and hard-to-find specialty spices and sauces. The storefront has ready-made lunch specials and paninis, tuna salad, and grilled-chicken sandwiches; you can also hire a chef from the company to cook full meals at your home, condo, or villa. For a premium, the company will deliver groceries, snacks, drinks, and fruit to wherever you are staying. ⊠ *Provo Golf Club, Grace Bay Rd., Grace Bay* ☎ *649/941–4141* ⊕ *www.gourmetcatering.tc.*

**Graceway Gourmet.** The Grace Bay branch of Provo's largest supermarket is likely to have what you're looking for. It's walkable from most of the resorts located right at the hub. It's especially popular for its prepared foods, which can be taken back and quickly reheated in your condo's kitchen when you don't feel like cooking from scratch. ⊠ *Dolphin Ave., Grace Bay* ☎ *649/333–5000* ⊕ *www.gracewaygourmet.com.*

**Kissing Fish Catering Co.** Kissing Fish Catering Co. has the same owners as Bay Bistro. The company will cater events like full-moon bonfires on the beach, weddings, and private parties, including beachside romantic dinners for two. Choose from pig roasts and ribs to four-course meals with beef Wellington, grouper with mango chutney, grilled lobster, or grilled chicken with sun-dried tomatoes, just to name a few from the extensive menu. If you're staying in a villa or condo with full kitchen, you can hire a personal chef to prepare meals in your kitchen. ⊠ *Sibonné Beach Hotel, Grace Bay Rd., at Bay Bistro, Grace Bay* ☎ *649/941–8917* ⊕ *www.kissingfish.tc.*

**Private Chef Turks and Caicos.** This company offers cooking lessons, prepared foods, or even a private chef to cook at your villa or condo and can also arrange and cater private beach functions. Chef Tadd has cooked around the world in places known for their fine restaurants, including Anguilla, New Orleans, and Chicago. Although you can't call, you can contact Chef Tadd by Skype: culinaryconceptstci. ✎ *tadd@culinaryconceptstci.com* ⊕ *privatecheftci.com.*

### HOME DECOR

**Inter Decor.** At this popular island interior-design store, you can find tropical shells, bookends, and fish vases. ⊠ *Saltmills Plaza, Grace Bay Rd., Grace Bay* ☎ *649/941–8717.*

### JEWELRY

**Jai's.** Jai's sells diamonds, perfumes, sunglasses, and watches, including the elusive blue diamond, which may remind you of Grace Bay. ⊠ *Regent Village, Regent St., Grace Bay* ☎ *649/941–4324* ⊕ *www.jais.tc.*

### SOUVENIRS

**Mama's.** Mama's is the place for the usual souvenirs and trinkets; you can also get your hair braided here. What really makes shopping fun is Mama herself, who may decide to sing a song or dance. ⊠ *Ports of Call Shopping Center, Grace Bay Rd., Grace Bay* ☎ *649/946–5538.*

**Silver Deep Boutique.** Silver Deep not only does excursions well but also has an awesome boutique. Tropical shirts, bathing suits, hats and sandals are just a small part of what the store carries; here you can buy carvings from the "Conch Man." ⊠ *Grace Bay Plaza, Grace Bay Rd., Grace Bay* ☎ *649/946–5612* ⊕ *www.silverdeep.com.*

## THE BIGHT

### JEWELRY

**Alicia Shulman Jewelry.** Alicia Shulman Jewelry makes handmade, bold, and beautiful jewelry that shows off your tan. Oversized semiprecious pearls, turquoise, and coral stones combine to make a statement. Shulman's designs are sold at the boutique at the Gansevoort Turks + Caicos; there are other branches at Seven Stars and at Parrot Cay. ⊠ *Gansevoort Turks + Caicos, Lower Bight Rd., The Bight* ☎ *649/946–5900* ⊕ *www.aliciashulman.com.*

## CLOSE UP

## Flamingos on Provo

Have you always wanted to see flamingos in their natural habitat? If so, then the Turks and Caicos is your place. There are a few hot spots that are better than others, but people get giddy when they come across a bright pink bird in a pond. On Provo, the best place to see them up close is at the golf course, though to do so you have to play a round of golf. But across the island, they are always a stone's throw away.

Behind the IGA supermarket on Leeward Highway is Flamingo Pond, a popular nesting ground, and if you drive all the way down to Turtle Tail you might get lucky with a sighting. North Caicos also has its own Flamingo Pond, with a small deck lookout, but you'll need binoculars to get a good look. And just across the causeway to Middle Caicos you'll stand a good chance of sighting flamingos up close if weather is favorable.

## TURTLE COVE

### ART AND CRAFT GALLERIES

**Greensleeves.** This boutique sells paintings and pottery by local artists, baskets, jewelry, and sisal mats and bags. The proceeds from sales of works in the Potcake Corner help fund the Potcake Place rescue center for the islands' stray dogs. ⊠ *Central Sq., Leeward Hwy., Turtle Cove* ☏ *649/946–4147.*

### LIQUOR

**Wine Cellar.** Visit this store for its large selection of duty-free liquor, at very good prices. ⊠ *Leeward Hwy., east of Suzie Turn Rd., Turtle Cove* ☏ *649/946–4536.*

## DISCOVERY BAY

### BOOKS

FAMILY **Unicorn Bookstore.** If you need to supplement your beach-reading stock or are looking for island-specific materials, visit the Unicorn for a wide assortment of books and magazines, lots of information and guides about the Turks and Caicos Islands and the Caribbean, and a large children's section with crafts, games, and art supplies. They also sell the cool PLS stickers for the back of your car. ⊠ *Leeward Hwy., in front of Graceway IGA Mall, Discovery Bay* ☏ *649/941–5458.*

### FOOD

**Graceway IGA.** With a large fresh-produce section, a bakery, gourmet deli, and extensive meat counter, the Provo's largest supermarket is likely to have what you're looking for. The most consistently well-stocked store on the island carries lots of known brands from the United Kingdom and North America, as well as a good selection of prepared foods, including rotisserie chicken, pizza, and potato salad. Expect prices to be much higher than at home. ⊠ *Leeward Hwy., Discovery Bay* ☎ *649/941–5000* ⊕ *www.gracewayiga.com.*

**Quality Supermarket.** When the IGA is out of stock, this fairly typical grocery store can sometimes fill the gaps. ⊠ *Discovery Bay* ☎ *649/941–7929.*

## DOWNTOWN

### FOOD

**Island Pride.** This often-overlooked supermarket carries lots of name brands, and it also has a Digicel phone store. ⊠ *Town Centre Mall, Old Airport Rd., Downtown* ☎ *649/941–3329.*

### JEWELRY

**Royal Jewels.** This chain sells gold and other jewelry, designer watches, perfumes, fine leather goods, and cameras—all duty-free. There are several other branches on the island, including one downtown in Arch Plaza. Two other branches are in Grace Bay at Beaches Turks and Caicos Villages and Spa and at Club Med Turkoise. ⊠ *Providenciales International Airport, Airport Rd., Downtown* ☎ *649/946–4699.*

### SOUVENIRS

**Turks and Caicos National Trust.** Buying the locally made ceramics, straw hats and bags, and small wooden sailboats sold at the Trust's shop helps raise money for this historic foundation. ⊠ *Towne Centre Mall, Butterfield Sq., Downtown* ☎ *649/946–5710* ⊕ *www.tcinationaltrust.com.*

# NIGHTLIFE

Although Provo is not known for its nightlife, there are some live bands and bars. Popular singers such as Mr. Blou (of NaDa fame), Just, Corey Forbes, and Quiton Dean perform at numerous restaurants and barbecue bonfires. Danny Bouy's, where you can always watch the latest game on big video screens, gets going late at night. Be sure to see if any ripsaw bands—aka rake-and-scrape—are playing while you're on the island; this is one of the quintessential local music types and is popular at local restaurants in Blue Hills.

The best late-night action can be found at the Gansevoort Turks + Caicos, where DJs play until the wee hours on weekends, and at Casablanca Casino, where everyone ends the night. If you want to see a show and dance until late, Club Med offers a night pass, which also includes drinks. But the best ambience is wherever Mr. Blou or Quinton Dean might be singing; both singers have huge followings—even among tourists. Quinton Dean has a huge fan base, including Prince, who picked him to go on his world tour.

On nights with major sports on TV, head to Gansevoort Turks + Caicos Beach Bar to watch on a huge TV in the sand.

The restaurant Somewhere On the Beach has happy hour every night and live music most nights at sunset. Danny Bouy's has nightly special happenings, including karaoke and live bands; there's something different every night. Locals end the evening with a mellow nightcap at Vino Tempo or the Vix, both at Regent Village. The rowdier crowd can be found at Jimmy's Dive Bar.

Keep abreast of events and specials by checking **TCI eNews** (⊕ *www.tcienews.com*) or **WhenWhereHow** (⊕ *www. WhereWhenHow.com*)

FULL-MOON PARTIES. Full moons are reputed to make people a little crazy. Bay Bistro usually has one at night on Grace Bay Beach, with a pig roast and tropical fare such as pineapple coleslaw. Bay Bistro's bonfire is a great hit with the kids, because you can roast marshmallows and make s'mores.

## RECOMMENDED BARS

**Danny Buoy's.** A popular Irish pub, Danny Buoy's has pool tables, darts, and big-screen TVs. It's a great place to watch sports broadcasts from all over. Different nights feature different nightlife; Tuesdays is karaoke, other nights have live music. It's open late every night. ⊠ *Grace Bay Rd., across from Carpe Diem Residences, Grace Bay* ☎ *649/946–5921* ⊕ *www.dannybuoys.com.*

## CASINOS

**Casablanca Casino.** The Casablanca Casino has brought slots, blackjack, American roulette, poker, craps, and baccarat back to Provo. Open daily until 4 am, this is the last stop for the night. ⊠ *Grace Bay Rd., Grace Bay* ☎ *649/941–3737.*

# AN EXCURSION TO WEST CAICOS

West Caicos is rich in history; pirates have hidden out here, using the island to ambush their enemies. One of the largest Spanish-galleon treasures was found in the waters that surround West Caicos. There's a rumor that Christopher Columbus's ship, the *Pinta*, is at the bottom of the sea here. West Caicos has the most attractive natural landscape of any island in the Turks and Caicos, with silver palms and ponds hosting bright-pink flamingos. There are old cotton-plantation ruins to explore. There are cliffs from which you can dive.

The best scuba diving in the area immediately surrounding Provo takes place in these waters; the corals drop off to more than 6,000 feet. So dramatic and instant is the drop-off that the water appears to be deep purple. Providenciales dive outfitters take divers to West Caicos as the premier dive location. But you have only three ways to come and enjoy West Caicos: via your own boat, with a dive company, or by excursion with Snuba.

# 3

# THE CAICOS
# AND THE CAYS

By
Ramona
Settle

**FEW VISITORS TO THE TURKS AND CAICOS** venture out from Provo, but when they do, they discover a whole other side to the islands. Most of the outlying cays are uninhabited, yet offer much for the adventurous explorer. You can also find cays that were pirate hideaways in the 17th and 18th centuries, now with resorts that take up the entire island. Most cays can be explored on day trips from Provo. The cays have endless beaches that you might have to yourself, with hidden coves where you can picnic while watching the boats go by, and many have small limestone cliffs with endless views of the ocean. Many are inhabited by friendly iguanas and circled by stingrays; if you are lucky, JoJo the dolphin might even swim with you. Surrounded by coral reefs, these waters were made for snorkeling, and the many reefs keep waves from crashing on shore, keeping the water calm like a lagoon. You can find cannons under the water and sand dollars to bring back home. South, North, and Middle Caicos offer a step back in time to rustic, lazy days in the sun. Pine Cay is rustic yet refined, laid-back yet charming. Parrot Cay was made for pampering, a day in the life of a movie star.

# PLANNING

## GETTING HERE AND AROUND

Most of the smaller islands between Providenciales and North Caicos can be reached only by boat from Provo. There is regularly scheduled ferry service between Provo and North Caicos, and from there you can drive across a causeway to Middle Caicos (about 90 minutes from the ferry landing by car). South Caicos can be reached only by plane. The Ambergris Cays are reachable only by private plane or boat.

## ABOUT THE HOTELS

Accommodations here are generally either in the budget category or very expensive, and you won't find many in the middle price ranges. You'll find several rustic, basic hotels and villas in South, North, and Middle Caicos; the owners are pleasant and helpful, and the towns are small and charming. All are clean and comfortable and offer air-conditioning, satellite TV, and home-cooked meals—everything that you could need to get away from it all. At the other end of the spectrum is pure pampering. Pine Cay

The Caicos
& the Cays

is like a luxury camp, quiet and relaxing, with a clubby atmosphere. Parrot Cay is one of the finest resorts in the world, where every need is anticipated and met—sorbet and cold bottled water by the pool and beach are placed in your hands seemingly before you even think about them. Throw in the best spa in the world, and relaxing doesn't get better than this.

## ABOUT THE RESTAURANTS

The outer islands don't offer much in the way of independent restaurants, and each island has only a handful of places to eat. Most of the Caicos Islands restaurants base menus on what was caught that day; some eating establishments are in private homes. You must call ahead—if you just show up, you might not get fed. The food in most of these places is simple island fare, served either in an indoor dining room or on an outdoor patio—often in the chef's own home. At Pine Cay food is included in your room rate, and the pool and beach setting combined with an outdoor grill make for fine casual meals. Parrot Cay, a private island retreat, has two elegant and upscale restaurants for guests to choose from. With advance reservations it's possible for nonguests to eat lunch at Pine Cay and Parrot Cay. Lunch will be expensive, but many travelers find that it's worth it for the chance to visit.

## PLANNING YOUR TIME

The smaller cays are reachable only by boat, most easily from Providenciales. Both Parrot Cay and Meridien Club have private ferries from Provo for their guests (and day-trippers). North Caicos is accessible by a ferry that runs several times a day from Provo. West Caicos is connected to North Caicos by a causeway, so both of these islands can be visited on a day trip from Provo. The other islands require more time. South Caicos is reachable by both a ferry and flights.

# LITTLE WATER CAY

*5 minutes by boat from Walkin' or Leeward marina.*

This small, uninhabited cay is a protected area under the Turks & Caicos National Trust and just a stone's throw away from Walkin' and Leeward marinas. On a private boat, the trip takes 5 minutes; an excursion boat takes 5 to 15 minutes once you leave the Grace Bay area. On these 150 acres are two trails, small lakes, red mangroves, and an abundance of native plants. Boardwalks protect the ground, and interpretive signs explain the habitat. The small island is home to about 2,000 rare, endangered rock iguanas. Experts say the iguanas are shy, but these creatures actually seem rather curious. They waddle right up to you, as if posing for a picture. Several water-sports operators from Provo and North Caicos include a stop on the island as a part of a snorkel or sailing excursion (it's usually called Iguana Island). There's a $5 permit fee to visit the cay, and the proceeds go toward conservation in the islands. ⚠ **Unless you're a woman who loves to get a pedicure the hard way, watch your toes when you're standing in sand near the iguanas—they have been known to mistake partially buried colored nails for grapes!**

### GETTING HERE

The only way to reach Little Water Cay is by organized excursion or private boat.

## TOP REASONS TO GO

**Day excursions.** All of Provo's excursion companies offer trips out to the cays. You can snorkel the reef, check out the iguanas at Little Water Cay, have a barbecue lunch on a secluded beach, and dive for conch all in one afternoon. On a full-day excursion you can go as far as Middle Caicos, where you can hike trails and explore caves. Keep an eye out for JoJo, the dolphin that's the unofficial mascot of Turks and Caicos and who may decide to join you.

**Parrot Cay.** Live like a rock star, if only for a day. Reservations are mandatory and not guaranteed, but if you can get here for lunch it's oh-so worth it—extravagant, but worth every penny. Lunch guests get access to the gor-geous beach, pool, and one of the best spas in the world.

**Pine Cay.** If you need to forget the worries of the day, this is your place. Call Le Meridian Club to set up the boat ride and lunch. Everything here is rustic and charming, laid-back and relaxing, and the beach is one of the best.

**Scuba South Caicos.** South Caicos is all about diving, as it's surrounded by coral walls that start at 30 feet and drop to more than 7,000 feet. The visibility here is the trump card: it's the best in the Turks and Caicos. The best way to dive South Caicos is from Salt Cay. Because you can't fly and dive on the same day, why not take an overnight at Salt Cay and discover its charms?

# PINE CAY

*15 to 20 minutes by boat from Provo.*

Pine Cay's 2½-mile-long (4-km-long) beach is among the most beautiful in the archipelago. The 800-acre private island, which is in the string of small cays between Provo and North Caicos, is home to a secluded resort and almost 40 private residences. The beach alone is reason to stay here: the sand seems a little whiter, the water a little brighter than beaches on the other cays.

Nonguests of the Meridian Club can make reservations for lunch, and boat transfer can be arranged for an extra cost; verify the total cost since it can vary. To bring costs down, make arrangements for one of the scheduled charters (usually when employees transfer to work) and spend the day enjoying the stunning beach. Ask what's on the menu first since it changes daily; Sunday usually features Cheeseburgers in Paradise.

**GETTING HERE**

The only way to reach Pine Cay is by private boat or on the Meridian Club resort's private ferry. If you're a guest of the resort and are staying for a week, one round-trip on the private shuttle is included in your rates. If you are not a resort guest, then the ferry costs $30 if you're going on a regular scheduled trip (up to $200 for a private charter) and you must make advance reservations.

## WHERE TO STAY

*For expanded hotel reviews, visit Fodors.com.*

★ Fodor's Choice ⊠ **Meridian Club.** *Resort.* Feeling like a private
$$$$ club, this resort on the prettiest beach in Turks and Caicos is *the* place to de-stress, with no phones, no TVs, no air-conditioning, no worries. **Pros:** the finest beach in Turks and Caicos; rates include some of the best food in the Turks and Caicos as well as snorkeling trips. **Cons:** no TVs or phones, so you are really unplugged here; expensive to get back to Provo for shopping or other Provo-based excursions or activities; all this simplicity costs a great deal. ⑤ *Rooms from: $1,060* ⊠ *Pine Cay* ☎ *649/946–7758, 866/746–3229* ⊕ *www.meridianclub.com* ⤴ *12 rooms, 1 cottage, 7 villas* ⊗ *Closed Aug.–Oct.* ⑩ *All meals.*

# FORT GEORGE CAY

*15 to 20 minutes by boat from Leeward Marina.*

An uninhabited cay and a protected national park, Fort George Cay was once a fortified island that protected the surrounding waters from pirates. Some of the 18th-century cannons that were put in place on the island are now underwater and can be viewed by snorkelers. The beach itself is stunning, a photographer's delight; the curved shoreline creates swirls of different shades of turquoise in the water; at low tide sandbars appear, and the blue-and-green water looks even brighter. This is a great spot to search for sand dollars, so bring a cookie tin so you can carry them back home. You can only collect white sand dollars; gray or dark ones are alive and illegal to take. All the excursion companies make stops here on their full-day trips, so ask if the island is on the itinerary of the boat you plan to take, either for snorkeling or a beach picnic.

The only way to reach Fort George Cay is by organized excursion or private boat.

# DELLIS CAY

*20 minutes by boat from Leeward Marina.*

This stunning small island, the second-to-last cay in the string of small islands between Providenciales and North Caicos, has a gorgeous sandy beach and good snorkeling; it's also a good place to search for sand dollars. It's currently uninhabited but looks ominous with its partially built Mandarin Oriental resort, which was abandoned when the economy tanked—its future is still uncertain at this writing—the shells of buildings can be seen from miles. If visiting by private boat, it's still worth a stop just for the many unusual seashells.

**GETTING HERE**
At this writing the only way to reach Dellis Cay is by private boat; excursion companies don't stop here anymore.

# PARROT CAY

*20 minutes by boat from Provo.*

The last in a string of small islands between Providenciales and North Caicos, Parrot Cay was once a hideout for pirate Calico Jack Rackham and his lady cohorts Mary Read and Anne Bonny. The 1,000-acre cay, between Fort George Cay and North Caicos, is now the site of an ultra-exclusive hideaway resort. If you're lucky enough to stay here, you'll have endless beautiful beaches and some small ruins to explore. Originally called Pirate Cay (because of the Spanish galleon treasures believed to be buried somewhere on the island), the island's name was changed to Parrot Cay when the resort was built.

Nonguests may eat lunch at the Lotus restaurant. Reservations are mandatory and may not be available during the busy periods, but if you go, it's a great day. And you may also visit the spa and pool.

## Suggested Beach Reads

Consider taking one of these books on your island vacation—it might amuse or even inspire you.

*A Trip to the Beach*, by Melinda Blanchard and Robert Blanchard, is about the adventures of opening their dream restaurant in paradise—in this case, a paradise called Anguilla.

*Don't Stop the Carnival: A Novel*, by Herman Wouk—who may be better known for his more serious novel *The Winds of War* or his play *The Caine Mutiny Court Martial*—is a comedy about living out your dreams on a tropical island.

*An Embarrassment of Mangos: A Caribbean Interlude*, by Ann Vanderhoof, follows a couple sailing through and surviving the Bahamas.

*The Carnival Never Got Started*, by S. Guy Lovelace, tells the tales and hardships of building a dream resort on an isolated island. The island is Salt Cay; the resort is the shuttered Windmills Plantation. The book is a haunting read, particularly because Hurricane Ike destroyed the colorful buildings in 2008.

### GETTING HERE

The only way to reach Parrot Cay is by private boat or the resort's private ferry from a private dock. If you are staying on Provo and would like to go to Parrot Cay for lunch or spa treatments, you must make a reservation and pay for your trip. The private ferry to Parrot Cay runs only for guests and resort workers returning home to Provo. With a reservation, your name will be added to the passenger list.

### WHERE TO STAY

*For expanded hotel reviews, visit Fodors.com.*

★ Fodor'sChoice ☒ **Parrot Cay Resort.** *Resort.* This private paradise, **$$$$** on its own island, pairs tranquillity with the best service in Turks and Caicos. **Pros:** impeccable service; gorgeous, secluded beach; the spa is considered one of the best in the world. **Cons:** only two restaurants on the entire island; it's expensive to get back and forth to Provo for excursions, as there is only private ferry service. ⑤ *Rooms from: $750* ☒ *Parrot Cay* ☎ *649/946-7788, 877/754-0726* ⊕ *www. comohotels.com/parrotcay* ⌘ *42 rooms, 4 suites, 14 villas* ⑩ *Breakfast.*

## SPAS

**Como Shambhala at Parrot Cay.** Asian holistic treatments, yoga with the world's leading teachers in a stunning pavilion, and a signature health-conscious cuisine are all part of the program here. The infinity pool, Pilates studio, steam room, sauna, and outdoor Jacuzzi make you feel complete. If you're staying in Provo, you can call for reservations, but you have to pay for the boat ride to Parrot Cay. Some consider this one of the finest spas in the world, and you'd be hard-pressed to find a better one in the Turks and Caicos. ✉ *Parrot Cay Resort, Parrot Cay* ☎ *649/946–7788* ⊕ *www. comoshambhala.com.*

# NORTH CAICOS

Thanks to abundant rainfall, this 41-square-mile (106-square-km) island is the lushest in the Turks and Caicos chain. With an estimated population of only 1,500, the expansive island allows you to get away from it all. Bird lovers can see a large flock of flamingos here; anglers can find shallow creeks full of bonefish; and history buffs can visit the ruins of a Loyalist plantation. Although there's little traffic, almost all the roads are paved, so bicycling is an excellent way to sightsee. Even though it's a quiet place, you can find some small eateries around the settlements and in Whitby, giving you a chance to try local and seafood specialties, sometimes served with homegrown okra or corn. The beaches are more natural here, and they are sometimes covered with seaweed and pine needles, as there are no major resorts to rake them daily. Nevertheless, some of these secluded strands are breathtaking, even if not as manicured as those of the upscale resorts on Provo.

North Caicos is definitely rustic, especially in comparison with shiny new Provo. Accommodations are clean but fairly basic. Locals are consistently friendly and life always seems to move slowly.

PHOTOGRAPHY TIP. Don't you hate finding that your pictures lack the bright colors you saw at the beach and on the water? Brightly lighted water reflects on the lens and causes the pictures to look washed out. Solution? Use a circular polarizer—it's like sunglasses for your camera, reducing glare and saturating colors so your pictures look professional.

### GETTING HERE

You can reach North Caicos from Provo with a daily ferry from S. Walkin & Sons Marina in Leeward; the trip takes about 30 minutes and makes several trips a day with the earliest leaving at 6:30 am (8:30 on Sunday) and the last returning at 5:30 pm (4:30 on Sunday). If you rent a car on North Caicos, you can even drive on the causeway to Middle Caicos (take it slow—it's filled with potholes). It's a great day trip from Provo.

Contacts **Caribbean Cruisin'** ⊠ *S. Walkin & Sons Marina, Heaving Down Rock, Leeward, Providenciales* ☎ *649/946–5406, 649/231–4191* ⊕ *www.tciferry.com.*

## EXPLORING NORTH CAICOS

**Flamingo Pond.** This is a regular nesting place for the beautiful pink birds. They tend to wander out into the middle of the pond, so bring binoculars to get a better look. ⊠ *North Caicos.*

**Kew.** This settlement has a small post office, a school, a church, and ruins of old plantations—all set among lush tropical trees bearing limes, papayas, and custard apples. Visiting Kew will give you a better understanding of the daily life of many islanders. ⊠ *North Caicos.*

**Three Mary Cays.** Three small rocks within swimming distance from Whitby Beach give you some of the best secluded snorkeling in all of the Turks and Caicos. You will often find ospreys nesting here, too. ⊠ *Off Whitby Beach.*

FAMILY **Wades Green.** Visitors can view well-preserved ruins of the greathouse, overseer's house, and surrounding walls of one of the most successful plantations of the Loyalist era. A lookout tower provides views for miles. Contact the National Trust for tour details. ⊠ *Kew* ☎ *649/941–5710 for National Trust* ⊕ *www.tcimall.tc/nationaltrust* 🎫 *$5* ⊗ *Daily, by appointment only.*

## WHERE TO EAT

✕ **Barracuda Beach Bar.** *Burger.* Though it's just a shack on the beach with a view, this is the epitome of what a Caribbean beach bar should be. And Susan, the owner, can definitely cook. While the food is casual—hamburgers, conch, etc.—the views are outstanding and the company even better. Hang out with the owners at sunset for stories of the way North Caicos used to be. You'll be in great

## All in the Family

Belongers, from the taxi driver meeting you at the airport to the chef feeding you, are often related. "Oh, him?" you will hear. "He my cousin!" Development has been mercifully slow here, so family connections, as well as crafts, bush medicine, ripsaw music, storytelling, and recipes, have remained constant. But where do such traditions come from? Recently, researchers came closer to finding out. Many Belongers had claimed that their great-great-grandparents had told them their forebears had come directly from Africa. For decades these stories were ignored. Indeed, most experts believed that Belongers were descendants of mostly second-generation Bermudian and Caribbean slaves.

In 2005 museum researchers continued their search for a lost slave ship called *Trouvadore*. The ship, which was wrecked off East Caicos in 1841, carried a cargo of 193 Africans, captured to be sold into slavery, almost all of whom miracu-

lously survived the wreck. As slavery had been abolished in this British territory at the time, all the Africans were found and freed in the Turks and Caicos islands. With only a few thousand inhabitants in the islands, these first-generation African survivors comprised about 7% of the population. Researchers have concluded that all the Belongers today may be linked by blood or marriage to this one incident.

During one expedition, divers found a wrecked ship of the right time period. If these remains are indeed the *Trouvadore,* the Belongers may finally have a physical link to their past to go with their cultural traditions. So while you're in the islands, look closely at the intricately woven baskets, listen carefully to the African rhythms in the ripsaw music, and savor the stories you hear. They may very well be the legacy of *Trouvadore* speaking to you from the past. For more information, check out ⊕ *www. slaveshiptrouvadore.com.*

company. ⑤ *Average main: $10* ⊠ *Pelican Beach Hotel* ☎ *649/946–7112* ⊕ *barracudabeachbar.blogspot.com.*

$ ╳ **Higgs Cafe.** *Caribbean.* Sometimes you get so caught up in the excitement of exploring isolated islands that you forget the basics, like food. With Higgs Cafe, located at the North Caicos Marina, now you won't go hungry for the day. It's open every day, and you can pick up native fare such oxtail, peas and rice, conch, and other locally caught fish; but regular American fare, including burgers

## Coming Soon

The buzz about Turks and Caicos has increased steadily since the turn of the millennium, a fact that hasn't missed the ears of developers. Several major hotel chains have set their horizons on Provo in particular; some of these are expected as early as 2014. Despite the recession, tourism to Provo is thriving. Other properties that were conceived just as the recession began have been abandoned for now, including the Tuscana on Providenciales, the Ritz-Carlton Molasses Reef on West Caicos, and the Mandarin Oriental on Dellis Cay. New restaurants seem to crop up every day. Grace Bay Club launched Stix, a beachside eatery where everything is served as kabobs, including dessert. And for the first time ever Provo now has Miss Moonies, a 24-hour convenience store, great for emergency staples in the middle of the night—or even a smoothie!

and hot dogs, is also available. It's casual fare on the go for exploring. $ *Average main: $12* ✉ *Sandy Point Marina* ☎ *649/946–7092* ⊗ *No dinner.*

$ ✕ **Last Chance Bar and Grill.** *Seafood.* A handmade wooden sign leads you to one of the best burgers on the island. Introduce yourself to Howard Gibbs, who bought this original 1930s home and lovingly restored it as a casual restaurant and bar. Light bites at lunch include hamburgers (did I say they were the best?) and fish fillets, are the simple offerings to eat while you explore North and Middle Caicos. At night, the choices include conch, fish, or shrimp with lemon butter and white wine sauce. Desserts are baked from scratch. Walk-ins for lunch are accepted, but reservations are needed for dinner. Howard is looking forward to a new dinner deck on a cliff overlooking the flats, which was still under construction at this writing. Cash only. $ *Average main: $14* ✉ *Bottle Creek* ☎ *649/232–4141* ⚓ *Reservations essential* ▭ *No credit cards.*

$$ ✕ **Silver Palm Restaurant.** *Eclectic.* Even on an isolated island you have to eat; fortunately, this North Caicos restaurant serves great food. If you're day-tripping from Provo, start with breakfast here, or call to order a picnic lunch to take with you as you explore. If you're staying on the island, dinner is highly recommended. The menu is varied, with plenty to please all tastes: grilled fish with lime, grilled chicken, and burgers on freshly baked bread. During lobster season try the half lobster tail or layered lobster sandwich at lunch. Reservations are required at dinner. It's actually

worth going to North Caicos just to eat here. ⑤*Average main: $17* ✉ *Whitby* ☎*649/946–7113* ⌕*Reservations essential* ⊘*Closed mid-June–mid-Nov.*

## WHERE TO STAY

*For expanded hotel reviews, visit Fodors.com.*

**$$** 🏨**Hollywood Beach Suites.** *Rental.* With 7 miles (11 km) of secluded beaches and few others to share them with, this property with four self-contained units is completely relaxing. **Pros:** secluded; tranquil; upscale furnishings. **Cons:** might feel a little quiet if you're after a busy vacation or active social scene. ⑤*Rooms from: $325* ✉ *Hollywood Beach Dr., Whitby* ☎*649/231–1020, 800/551–2256* ⊕*www.hollywoodbeachsuites.com* ⟿*4 suites* ⦿*No meals.*

**$** 🏨**Pelican Beach Hotel.** *Hotel.* North Caicos islanders Susan and Clifford Gardiner built this small, palmetto-fringed hotel in the 1980s on the quiet, mostly deserted Whitby Beach. **Pros:** the beach is just outside your room; linens are crisp and clean. **Cons:** location may be too remote and sleepy for some people; beach is in a natural state, meaning seaweed and pine needles. ⑤*Rooms from: $165* ✉ *Whitby* ☎*649/946–7112, 877/774–5486* ⊕*www.pelicanbeach.tc* ⟿*14 rooms, 2 suites* ⊘*Closed Aug. 15–Sept. 15* ⦿*Some meals.*

## BEACHES

The beaches of North Caicos are superb for shallow snorkeling and sunset strolls, and the waters offshore have excellent scuba diving.

**Horse Stable Beach.** Horse Stable Beach is the main beach for annual events and beach parties. **Amenities:** none. **Best for:** solitude; walking. ✉*North Caicos.*

**Sandy Point Beach.** Sandy Point is a gorgeous strand, now taken over by Royal Reef Resort construction. Most of the strands have no development on them, leaving the beaches in a more natural state. **Amenities:** none. **Best for:** solitude. ✉*North Caicos.*

**Whitby Beach.** Whitby Beach usually has a gentle tide, and its thin strip of sand is bordered by palmetto plants and taller trees. **Amenities:** food and drink. **Best for:** solitude; walking. ✉ *Whitby.*

# MIDDLE CAICOS

At 48 square miles (124 square km) and with fewer than 300 residents, this is the largest yet least developed of the inhabited islands in the Turks and Caicos chain. A limestone ridge runs to about 125 feet above sea level, creating dramatic cliffs on the north shore and a cave system farther inland. Middle Caicos has rambling trails along the coast; the Crossing Place Trail, which is maintained by the National Trust, follows the path used by the early settlers to go between the islands. Inland are quiet settlements with friendly residents.

North Caicos and Middle Caicos are now linked by a causeway, so it's possible to take a ferry from Provo to North Caicos, rent a car, and explore both North Caicos and Middle Caicos in a single day if you get an early start.

### GETTING HERE

The only way to reach Middle Caicos is by car (over the causeway that connects it to North Caicos). Air Turks & Caicos no longer offers flights.

## EXPLORING MIDDLE CAICOS

FAMILY  **Conch Bar Caves.** These limestone caves have eerie underground lakes and milky-white stalactites and stalagmites. Archaeologists have discovered Lucayan artifacts in the caves and the surrounding area. The caves are now inhabited only by some harmless bats. If you visit, don't worry— they don't bother visitors. It's best to get a guide. If you tour the caves, be sure to wear sturdy shoes, not sandals. ✉ *Middle Caicos.*

## WHERE TO EAT

**$$**  ✕ **Daniel's Cafe.** *Seafood.* Chef Daniel and his son Devon opened this café to serve the island's 250 full-time residents as well as day-trippers from North Caicos and Provo. The outdoor deck has beautiful views of Mudjin Harbour and the ocean. Food is simple and fresh: conch, fish, peas and rice, and salads with homemade baked bread. The restaurant is also home to the nonprofit Middle Co-Op Shop, which promotes all things made locally, from bags and hats to hand-carved sailboats used every year at the Valentine's Day Cup at Bamberra Beach. Reservations are required for the three-course dinner, which fills up quickly. ⑤ *Average main: $17* ✉ *Mudjin Harbour* ☎ *649/946–6132* ⊘ *Closed Mon.*

## NORTH CAICOS IN A DAY

You must prearrange a car for any visit to North Caicos; someone will be waiting at the Sandy Point ferry dock and will give you a map. Avoid Sunday, though, as many places are closed. From Provo, take the ferry from Walkin Marina; it takes about 25 minutes.

From the dock road, take your first right. This road ends in a "T" and faces a building with a bright blue roof; you'll turn here on your way back. At this intersection, take a right to Kew Town.

If you go left and loop around, you come to the Wades Green Plantation ruins. If you want to see the plantation, you need to make arrangements in advance; otherwise, the entrance will be chained. These are the best ruins in TCI, so it's worth making the call.

Go back to the blue-roofed building, and keep driving until the road ends. At this "T" you will have signs facing you that say "Silver Palms" with arrows. Take a left toward Silver Palms, where you can check out Whitby Beach. Continue past the circle—the road gets rough but only for a short distance, then becomes paved again. You will see gorgeous homes on the right; the beachfront here is Pumpkin Bluff. Stay to the

right, and the road turns into packed sand with potholes, but you can navigate it easily if you drive slowly. You will see a small sign to turn to Three Mary Cays, one of the best snorkeling spots in TCI.

Going back, stay straight past the Silver Palms sign. On the right you will see Flamingo Pond, worth a stop to spot flamingos. Otherwise, continue straight to Bottle Creek settlement, where the turquoise views of the off-shore flats are enough reason to make this drive. Stop at Last Chance to have lunch and meet Howard. If you are going on to Middle Caicos, then just keep going straight to the causeway.

When you return to the ferry dock, on the right you'll see a leg-high sign to Pelican Beach Resort, which has Barracuda's Beach Bar. This casual bar on Whitby Beach should be your last stop before returning to the ferry. After your refreshment break, take a left at Silver Palms sign, then a right at the blue-roofed building back to the ferry.

If you're combining a trip to both North and Middle Caicos, save Three Mary Cays, Kew Town, and Wades Green Plantation for another trip. You'll need the extra time to see a bit of Middle Caicos.

★ **Fodor**$Choice ✕ **Mudjin Bar and Grill.** *Caribbean.* The view alone from the outside deck overlooking Mudjin Harbour Beach makes a meal here worthwhile. As a bonus, the food is also great, with the presentation just as beautiful as the setting. Standouts for lunch are the mini-lobster clubs with pineapple and avocado mayo (in season), sweet potato conch fritters with balsamic reduction and roasted garlic aioli, and pulled pork sandwiches with caramelized island fruit. For dinner try the chipotle southern fried chicken or the fish ceviche with pico de gallo. Prices are less than you would pay in Provo, though the quality of the food is just as good as that in more upscale and expensive restaurants. Walk-ins are fine for lunch, but reservations for dinner are essential. ⑤ *Average main: $15* ✉ *Blue Horizon Resort, Mudjin Harbour* ☎ *649/946–6141* ♿ *Reservations essential* ⊘ *Closed Sun.*

## WHERE TO STAY

*For expanded hotel reviews, visit Fodors.com.*

★ **Fodor**$Choice ☖ **Blue Horizon Resort.** *Hotel.* At this property,
**$$** undulating cliffs skirt one of the most dramatic beaches in the Turks and Caicos. **Pros:** breathtaking views of Mudjin Harbour from the rooms; lack of development makes you feel like you're away from it all. **Cons:** need a car to explore; probably too isolated for some; three-night minimum. ⑤ *Rooms from: $290* ✉ *Mudjin Harbour* ☎ *649/946–6141* ⊕ *www.bhresort.com* ⛵ *5 cottages, 2 villas* ⦿ *No meals.*

## BEACHES

Middle Caicos is blessed with two particularly stunning beaches: Mudjin Harbour and Bamberra Beach.

**Bamberra Beach.** Each summer Bamberra Beach hosts the Middle Caicos Model Sailboat Race. The hand-carved boats are painted in bright colors and can be purchased at the Middle Caicos Co-Op Shop in Blue Hills in Provo. **Amenities:** none. **Best for:** solitude; walking. ✉ *Middle Caicos.*

**Mudjin Harbour Beach.** You can hike the trails on the cliffs overlooking Mudjin Harbour and find small private coves. The beach is divided by coral that sticks out of the water; on one side the sea is calm, on the other side, the waves crash over the coral. At low tide, sandbars form in the middle. **Amenities:** food and drink. **Best for:** walking; sunset. ✉ *Mudjin Harbour.*

**Wild Cow Run.** If you're feeling adventurous and want an amazing strand all to yourself, check out Wild Cow Run. Numerous sandbars form at low tide. Chances are you'll have it all to yourself—it's out of the way and hard to find. **Amenities:** none. **Best for:** solitude; walking. ⊠ *Middle Caicos*.

## SPORTS AND THE OUTDOORS

### CAVE TOURS

**Cardinal Arthur.** Although exploring Middle Caicos on your own can be fun, a guided tour with Cardinal can illuminate the island's secret spots, from caves to the spots where flamingos flock. He can also show you the sandbars that make vacationers giddy and that can't be found by car. By skiff he can show off all the hidden beaches reached only by water, too. ☎ *649/946–6107*.

# SOUTH CAICOS

This 8½-square-mile (21-square-km) island with a population of only 1,400 was once an important salt producer; today it's the heart of the country's fishing industry. You'll find long, white beaches; jagged bluffs; quiet backwater bays; and salt flats. The island is so basic and rustic that you may feel as if you are stepping back in time to a sleepier world, where you have to stop the car to allow donkeys and cows to cross the street.

You will see construction all over the island (two resorts are under development at this writing). As your plane lands, you can't miss the construction site for the Caicos Beach Club Resort & Marina sitting perched on a hill; it has changed developers several times and was first scheduled to open in 2005. Now seven buildings are in various stages of completion (the clubhouse is finished), so some progress is being made. When finished, the resort will be huge, with some 700 rooms, a casino, and a marina. A 200-room resort is also being built on East Bay Beach.

In 2008 Hurricanes Hanna and Ike gave South Caicos a one–two punch, and many of the buildings at Cockburn Harbour sustained substantial damage; island residents had to wait more than a month to have power restored. Although the island has recovered, the few dive operators have disappeared. The best way to dive (other than independently) is through Sea Crystal Divers from Salt Cay (this requires spending the night in Salt Cay because dive trips originate there).

## A DAY IN MIDDLE CAICOS

After picking up your car from the ferry in North Caicos, head straight for the causeway to Middle Caicos. The trip from the ferry dock to Bamberra Beach takes about 90 minutes. Once you're on the causeway, it's straight forward because there is only one main road on Middle Caicos (there's a small settlement with a couple of turns, but all roads eventually lead back to the main highway). Bamberra beach has tiki huts, and at low tide you can even walk out to a small cay. There's a small leg-high sign that says "Bamberra Beach" on the left. Follow the sandy path (a regular car will be just fine) until you can see the beach ahead. Bring bug spray.

On your way back to North Caicos, stop at Daniel's Cafe for a local lunch of fish or conch. Introduce yourself to him and his son Devon; both are delightful to talk to. You can also have lunch at the new restaurant overlooking Mudjin Harbour at Blue Horizon Resort. Mudjin Harbour is the real prize on Middle Caicos, and no matter how many times you make this trip, you have to stop here. There are signs for "Blue Horizon Resort" where you park.

Close to the resort are the Conch Bar Caves, which you can explore, but a guide is highly recommended because the caves are dark and slippery, and there are bats.

After enjoying Mudjin Harbour Beach, stop at Barracuda Beach Bar at the Pelican Beach Hotel for a drink, and check out Whitby Bay. Stop at Flamingo Pond to see if you can spot any pink flamingos before you return to the ferry.

If this is your second trip, you should continue driving past Bamberra Beach on Middle Caicos and keep going until you see a settlement called Lorimar. Take a left before the "Lorimar" sign. Follow the road until you get to a roundabout, where you should take the first right. Follow the road for about 15 minutes until the packed sand becomes loose; don't drive too far because it becomes too sandy to drive a regular car. Park and walk to your left; you'll be at Wild Cow Run, which is amazing. You will have this beach, which goes on for miles, to yourself; on one end many little sandbars form at low tide, when you can walk out to Joe Grants Cay. Keep an eye on the time when you're here because it flies. Be sure to bring water because there's nothing close by. Always finish your trip with a stop at Mudjin Harbour before returning to the ferry.

The major draw for South Caicos is its excellent diving and snorkeling on the pristine wall and reefs (with an average visibility of 100 feet). This is a treat enjoyed by only a few, but it's practically the only thing to do on South Caicos other than to lie on the lovely beaches. Several local fishermen harvest spiny lobsters for the Turks and Caicos and for export. Making up the third-largest reef in the world, the coral walls surrounding South Caicos are dramatic, dropping dramatically from 50 feet to 6,000 feet in the blink of an eye.

### GETTING HERE

The only way to reach South Caicos is by air on a flight from Provo on Air Turks & Caicos, or by boat from Salt Cay, which is operated by Cindy Herwin of Salt Cay Whale Watching.

Airline Contacts **Air Turks & Caicos** ☎ 649/941–5481 ⊕ *www.airturksandcaicos.com*.

---

## EXPLORING SOUTH CAICOS

At the northern end of the island are fine white-sand beaches; the south coast is great for scuba diving along the drop-off; and there's excellent snorkeling off the windward (east) coast, where large stands of elkhorn and staghorn coral shelter several varieties of small tropical fish. Spiny lobster and queen conch are found in the shallow Caicos Bank to the west, and are harvested for export by local processing plants. The bonefishing here is some of the best in the West Indies. The settlement is called Cockburn Harbour, and it hosts the South Caicos Regatta, held each year in May.

**Boiling Hole.** Abandoned salinas (natural salt pans) make up the center of this island—the largest, across from the downtown ballpark, receives its water directly from an underground source connected to the ocean through this "boiling" hole. ✉ *South Caicos*.

---

## WHERE TO EAT

Restaurant choices on South Caicos are limited, and no one takes credit cards, so bring cash. Except for the Dolphin Pub at the South Caicos Ocean & Beach Resort, the three best places are operated directly out of the owner's homes. Love's restaurant (on Airport Road) offers a daily changing menu of fresh seafood priced from $8 to $15. Darryl's (on Stubbs Road) is another casual restaurant that offers whatever is brought in for the day; expect to pay $10 to $20. Ask around to find out when (or if) these local favorites will be open; neither has a phone.

**$$** ✕**Dolphin Pub.** *Eclectic.* The only real restaurant on the island serves casual, crowd-pleasing food: you'll find burgers, chicken, and fish. There is some Asian influence in the sauces and rice, and there are certainly Caribbean influences in the jerk sauce on the fish. At night this turns into a gathering place for guests to tell their tales about the sea, the fish that they caught, or the sea eagle ray that they spotted while diving. If you are around for lunch (most visitors to South Caicos will be scuba diving), this is your only choice. ⑤*Average main: $15* ✉*South Caicos Ocean & Beach Resort, Turker Hill* ☎*649/946–3810.*

## WHERE TO STAY

At this writing there's only one place to stay on South Caicos, but that may change if the two resorts under development are ever finished.

*For expanded hotel reviews, visit Fodors.com.*

⌂**South Caicos Ocean & Beach Resort.** *Hotel.* Rustic and basic—though perfectly acceptable—this is your only lodging option in South Caicos at this writing. **Pros:** each room has stunning views of the Caicos Banks; the best scuba diving off South Caicos is in front of the hotel; it has the only real restaurant on the island. **Cons:** you need cash for everything but your room; not on the beach; no dive shop at the resort. ⑤*Rooms from: $125* ✉*Turker Hill* ☎*649/946–3810* ⊕*southcaicos.oceanandbeachresort.com* ↩*24 rooms, 6 apartments* ⦿*No meals.*

## BEACHES

**Belle Sound.** The beaches at Belle Sound on South Caicos will take your breath away, with lagoonlike waters. Expect the beach to be natural and rustic—after storms you will see some seaweed. **Amenities:** none. **Best for:** walking. ✉*South Caicos.*

**East Caicos.** To the north of South Caicos uninhabited East Caicos has a beautiful 17-mile (27-km) beach on its north coast. The island was once a cattle range and the site of a major sisal-growing industry. East Caicos is only accessible by boat (most easily from Middle Caicos). **Amenities:** none. **Best for:** solitude; walking; swimming. ✉*South Caicos.*

# 3

## A Tail of a Dive

CLOSE UP

In the 1970s, during the height of drug-running days, planes from Colombia landed all the time on South Caicos. One plane, a Convair 29A (the size of a DC-3), ran out of gas as it approached the runway. The pilot survived, but the plane did not. The wings and body stayed intact, the nose and tail broke off as the plane crashed into the ocean. The pieces now sit in about 50 feet of water, and they are almost completely encrusted with coral. The dive site is in two parts: "The Plane" is the main hub with the body and wings; the "Warhead" is the tail of the wreck a few yards away. Usually there are schools of snapper and Jacks swimming through the wreck, and at night, sometimes sharks, making it a unique dive. As you land at the airport, you can see the wreck from the air. Hurricane Ike did more damage to the plane in 2008, but it still makes an interesting dive site.

**Little Ambergris Cay.** Due south of South Caicos is Little Ambergris Cay, an uninhabited cay about 14 miles (23 km) beyond the Fish Cays, with excellent bonefishing on the second-largest sandbar in the world. **Amenities:** none. **Best for:** solitude. ⊠ *South Caicos.*

**Long Bay.** On the opposite side of the ridge from Belle Sound, Long Bay is an endless stretch of beach, but it can be susceptible to rough surf; however, on calmer days, you'll feel like you're on a deserted island. **Amenities:** parking (free); water sports. **Best for:** solitude; walking; windsurfing. ⊠ *South Caicos.*

## SPORTS AND THE OUTDOORS

### DIVING

The reef walls that surround South Caicos are part of the third-largest reef system in the world. The reef starts at about 50 feet and then drops dramatically to around 6,000 feet. Most sights on the walls have no names, but you can dive anywhere along them. The visibility is ideal—consistently more than 100 feet and most times beyond that.

The **Caves** on Long Cay (which you can see out your window at the South Caicos Ocean & Beach Resort) are really five caves under the water that were made for exploring. The **Maze,** suitable only for expert divers, will keep you swimming at 105 feet through tunnels before you pop out at 75 feet. The **Arch,** so named because it resembles the kind of natural bridge found on Aruba (only under the water) offers the opportunity to see both eagle rays and sharks.

The **Blue Hole** is similar to the Blue Hole in Belize, but this one is under the ocean rather than on land. It's a natural sinkhole in the middle of the ocean between Middle Caicos and South Caicos on the Caicos Banks that drops to 250 feet. From the air, it looks like a dark blue circle in the middle of a turquoise sea.

Sharks, barracuda, octopus, green morays, eagle rays, and lobster are only some of the sea creatures that are common to these waters. During whale-watching season from mid-January to mid-April you can watch adult whales teach their babies how to clean themselves on the sand patches within view of South Caicos Ocean & Beach Resort.

At this writing, no dive operators are working on South Caicos. Your best bet is to find a dive operator who will come over from Salt Cay.

### FISHING

**Beyond the Blue.** Beyond the Blue offers bonefishing charters on a specialized airboat, which can operate in less than a foot of water. Lodging packages are available. ☎ 649/231–1703 ⊕ www.beyondtheblue.com.

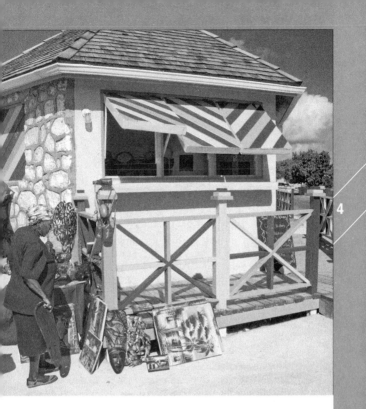

# GRAND TURK

By
Ramona
Settle

**SLEEPY, LAID-BACK, LAZY, AND CHARMING,** Grand Turk is the kind of place that you either love or can't wait to leave. Rich in history, the island's historic buildings were made mostly from scraps of the ships of pirates who were tricked into coming ashore. Locals walk slowly down the street in the heat of the sun, wearing big floppy hats or under parasols. Perfectionists and guests who want the latest and trendiest may not appreciate the island's rustic, laid-back charm, but photographers and divers delight in the colors and authentic ambience, and vacationers looking to simply relax will find much to like about Grand Turk.

Just 7 miles (11 km) long and a little more than 1 mile (2½ km) wide, this island, with a population of 3,700, is the capital and seat of the Turks and Caicos government. It has been a longtime favorite destination of divers eager to explore the 7,000-foot-deep pristine coral walls that drop down only 300 yards out to sea. On shore, the tiny, quiet island has white-sand beaches, the national museum, and a small population of wild horses and donkeys, which meander past the white-walled courtyards, pretty churches, and bougainvillea-covered colonial inns on their daily commute into town. History here mixes with nature.

Many argue that Grand Turk was the actual first landfall during Christopher Columbus's first voyage to the New World—not the Bahamas, which has always been the traditional location. You will see national park signs making this claim all along Front Street. The island first gained international recognition in 1962, when John Glenn's Mercury spacecraft splashed down nearby after he became the first astronaut to orbit the Earth. You can see a replica of his rocket ship outside the airport.

A cruise-ship complex that opened at the southern end of the island in 2006 now brings some 600,000 visitors per year. Despite the dramatic changes this could have made to this peaceful tourist spot, the dock is pretty much self-contained, and is about 3 miles (5 km) from the tranquil, small hotels of Cockburn Town, Pillory Beach, and the Ridge, and far from most of the western-shore dive sites. The influx of tourists has had a mostly positive effect on the island, pushing Grand Turk to open up a few new historic sites, including Grand Turk's old prison and the lighthouse. Otherwise, the atmosphere is pretty much the same.

In September 2008 Grand Turk was devastated by a one–two punch from Hurricanes Hanna and Ike. As luck would have it, the reefs did not suffer any serious damage, and divers were back in the waters in a few days. Except for some ongoing construction on Front Street, you'd never know it happened.

# PLANNING

## GETTING HERE AND AROUND

### AIR TRAVEL

Unless you're arriving on a cruise ship, you'll need to fly to Grand Turk from Provo on Air Turks & Caicos, which currently has the only scheduled flights here. There are no scheduled ferries.

### CAR TRAVEL

If you're staying anywhere on Duke Street or Front Street, you can easily walk to some of the beaches, to excursion companies, and to the best restaurants. You'll need a car if you want to explore beyond town; the local car-rental agency is Tony's Rental Cars. Another option is to rent a golf cart from Nathan's Golf Cart Rentals, which is at the cruise port; on cruise days these are usually taken by cruise passengers. The island is small enough that a golf cart works, but a rental costs $80 for the day. On days when there's no ship in port, call before reaching Grand Turk, and Nathan will meet you at the airport.

## ESSENTIALS

### HOTELS

Don't come to Grand Turk expecting five-star resorts with full service and amenities. The first tourists on the island were divers who didn't require much from lodgings. Most accommodations are bed-and-breakfasts or small, humble homes. Some are in historic mansions, and there are a few small hotels. All are clean and comfortable, and offer all the updates you have come to expect when traveling.

### RESTAURANTS

The restaurants here are small and charming, used as gathering places. Most are set either in courtyards under huge trees and flowering bushes, or next to the beach with sweeping views. Most places are associated with hotels or other lodgings. The chefs know how to turn the fresh catch into

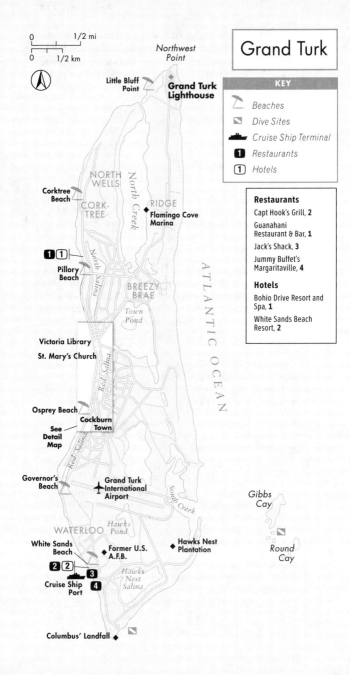

# Grand Turk

*Northwest Point*

Little Bluff Point

**Grand Turk Lighthouse**

## KEY

- Beaches
- Dive Sites
- Cruise Ship Terminal
- **1** Restaurants
- **1** Hotels

### Restaurants

Capt Hook's Grill, **2**

Guanahani Restaurant & Bar, **1**

Jack's Shack, **3**

Jummy Buffet's Margaritaville, **4**

### Hotels

Bohio Drive Resort and Spa, **1**

White Sands Beach Resort, **2**

0 — 1/2 mi
0 — 1/2 km

NORTH WELLS

Corktree Beach

CORK-TREE

RIDGE

North Creek

Flamingo Cove Marina

**1 1**

Pillory Beach

North Salina

BREEZY BRAE

Town Pond

ATLANTIC OCEAN

Victoria Library

St. Mary's Church

Red Salina

Osprey Beach

**Cockburn Town**

See Detail Map

Red Salina

Governor's Beach

Grand Turk International Airport

South Creek

*Gibbs Cay*

*Round Cay*

WATERLOO

*Hawks Pond*

White Sands Beach

Former U.S. A.F.B.

Hawks Nest Plantation

**2 2** **3**

Cruise Ship Port

**4**

*Hawks Nest Salina*

Columbus' Landfall

fine dining; the ambience is laid-back and relaxing. At the end of the day most restaurants turn into nightlife venues, where people gather to talk of their underwater sightings.

# EXPLORING GRAND TURK

Circling the island is easy, because it's only 7 miles (11 km) long and only 1 mile (2½ km) wide. On a day trip you can have fun for a couple of hours and still have time to relax in the sun the same afternoon. Stroll down Front Street with its historic buildings, making sure to stop in the excellent museum. If there's a cruise ship in port, check out the old prison and go to the lighthouse. Dive the crystal-clear waters or feed the stingrays at Gibb's Cay. People-watch and do some light shopping at the cruise port. End the day at the Sand Bar with tales of your adventures. Those with more time will be able to relax and see the island's sights and enjoy its beautiful beaches and dive sites at their leisure.

Pristine beaches with vistas of turquoise waters, small local settlements, historic ruins, and native flora and fauna are among the sights on Grand Turk. About 3,700 people live on this 7½-square-mile (19-square-km) island, and it's hard to get lost, as there aren't many roads.

## COCKBURN TOWN

The buildings in the colony's capital and seat of government reflect a 19th-century Bermudian style. Narrow streets are lined with low stone walls and old street lamps, which are now powered by electricity. The once-vital salinas (natural salt pans, where the sea leaves a film of salt) have been restored, and covered benches along the sluices offer shady spots for observing wading birds, including flamingos that frequent the shallows. Be sure to pick up a copy of the tourist board's Heritage Walk guide to discover Grand Turk's rich architecture.

**Her Majesty's Prison.** This prison was built in the 19th century to house runaway slaves and slaves who survived the wreck of the *Trouvadore* in 1841. After the slaves were granted freedom, the prison housed criminals and even modern-day drug runners until it closed in the 1990s. The last hanging here was in 1960. Now you can see the cells, solitary-confinement area, and exercise patio. The prison is open only when there is a cruise ship at the port. ⊠ *Pond St., Cockburn Town.*

## TOP REASONS TO GO

**History.** It's surprising how such a small island can have so much history. Travel to the lighthouse, visit the old prison where the last hanging was as recent as 1960, and certainly visit the national museum; you'll be smarter by the time you go back to the beach.

**Dive the Wall.** The coral walls drop off to thousands of feet as little as 300 feet offshore in Grand Turk—it's even possible to swim to the wall from the beach. The less time it takes to reach the site, the more time to enjoy your dive.

**Old Caribbean Charm.** In Grand Turk you'll feel like you've stepped back in time. Giving meaning to "island time," locals just take it slow. On Front Street layers of sun-bleached, peeling paint only add to the charm. Walk down the street and everyone smiles and says hello; some will even stop to converse and are truly interested in

where you're from. Watch where you walk; you'll share the road with wild donkeys and roosters.

**Shopping and Playing at the Cruise Port.** So you think you can't mix Old Caribbean charm with a 3,000-passenger cruise ship? The beauty of Grand Turk is that despite its small size, these two happily coexist, and fickle vacationers can have it both ways: the relaxation of a slower life, and 3 miles (5 km) away, the bustle of shops and pool games. But the bustle is only bustling (and available) when there is a cruise ship at the dock.

**Gibbs Cay.** A 20-minute boat ride from Front Street takes you along the shore to an un-inhabited cay for snorkeling; in another 5 minutes you're in Gibbs Cay. The stingrays already sense the boat coming, and they will swim with you the whole time you are there. It's a don't-miss experience.

FAMILY **Turks and Caicos National Museum.** In one of the oldest stone buildings on the islands, the national museum houses the Molasses Reef wreck, the earliest shipwreck—dating to the early 1500s—discovered in the Americas. The natural-history exhibits include artifacts left by Taíno, African, North American, Bermudian, French, and Latin American settlers. The museum has a 3-D coral reef exhibit, a walk-in Lucayan cave with wooden artifacts, and a gallery dedicated to Grand Turk's little-known involvement in the Space Race (John Glenn made landfall here after being the first American to orbit the Earth). An interactive children's gallery keeps knee-high visitors "edutained." The museum also claims that Grand Turk was where Columbus first landed in the New World. The most original display is a collection of messages in bottles that have washed ashore from all over the world. ✉ *Duke St., Cockburn Town* ☎ *649/946–2160* ⊕ *www.tcmuseum.org* 💲 *$5* ⊙ *Mon., Tues., Thurs., and Fri. 9–4; Wed. 9–5; Sat. 9–1.*

## NORTH RIDGE

**Grand Turk Lighthouse.** More than 150 years ago, the lighthouse, built in the United Kingdom and transported piece by piece to the island, protected ships from wrecking on the northern reefs. Use this panoramic landmark as a starting point for a breezy cliff-top walk by following the donkey trails to the deserted eastern beach. ✉ *Lighthouse Rd., North Ridge.*

# BEACHES

Visitors to Grand Turk will be spoiled when it comes to beach options: sunset strolls along miles of deserted beaches, picnics in secluded coves, beachcombing on the coralline sands, snorkeling around shallow coral heads close to shore, and admiring the impossibly turquoise-blue waters. There are small cove beaches in front of Crabtree Apartments and the Osprey Beach Hotel that you will have pretty much to yourself. The best of the small beaches is next to the Sand Dollar Bar and in front of Oasis Dive Shop; it's also an excellent place for snorkeling right off the beach. The long stretch starting at the Grand Turk Cruise Terminal Beach, followed by White Sands Beach, and ending at Governor's Beach allows miles of walking and beachcombing.

## COCKBURN TOWN

**Governor's Beach.** A beautiful crescent of powder-soft sand and shallow, calm turquoise waters front the official British governor's residence, called Waterloo, framed by tall casuarina trees that provide plenty of natural shade. To have it all to yourself, go on a day when cruise ships are not in port (but bring your own water). On days when ships are in port, the beach is lined with lounge chairs, and bars and restaurants are open. **Amenties:** parking (free); toilets. **Best for:** swimming; walking. ✉ *Cockburn Harbour.*

## PILLORY BEACH

**Pillory Beach.** With sparkling neon turquoise water, this is the prettiest beach on Grand Turk; it also has great off-the-beach snorkeling. **Amenities:** food and drink; parking (free); toilets. **Best for:** snorkeling; swimming; walking. ⊠ *Pillory Beach.*

## GRAND TURK CRUISE TERMINAL

**White Sands Beach.** White Sands Beach has sparkling water that offers more seclusion from the cruise crowds yet access to the terminal and shops (they are open only when a ship is in port). The old weathered fishing boats parked on the beach contrast with the big shiny cruise ships that park behind them. **Amenities:** food and drink; parking (free). **Best for:** partiers; swimming; walking. ⊠ *Between the cruise terminal and Governor's Beach, Grand Turk Cruise Terminal.*

# WHERE TO EAT

Conch in every shape and form, fresh grouper, and lobster (in season) are the favorite dishes at the laid-back restaurants that line Duke Street. Away from these more touristy areas, smaller and less expensive eateries serve chicken and ribs, curried goat, peas and rice, and other native island specialties. Prices are more expensive than in the United States, as most of the produce has to be imported.

## COCKBURN TOWN

**$$$** × **Birdcage Restaurant.** *Caribbean.* This has become the place to be on Sunday and Wednesday nights, when a sizzling barbecue of ribs, chicken, and lobster combines with live "rake-and-scrape" music from a local group called High Tide to draw an appreciative crowd. Arrive before 8 pm to secure beachside tables and an unrestricted view of the band; the location around the Osprey pool is lovely. The rest of the week, enjoy more elegant and eclectic fare accompanied by a well-chosen wine list. ⑤ *Average main: $24* ⊠ *Osprey Beach Hotel, Duke St., Cockburn Town* ☎ *649/946–2666* ⊕ *www.ospreybeachhotel.com/dining.*

**$$** × **Mookie Pookie Pizza Palace.** *Pizza.* Local husband-and-wife team "Mookie" and "Pookie" have created a wonderful backstreet restaurant that has gained well-deserved popularity over the years as much more than a pizza place. At

# Cockburn Town

0 ——— 200 yrds
0 ——— 200 meters

**Turks & Caicos 1**
**National Museum**

*Salina*

**Turks & Caicos**
**Tourist Board** *i*

**Her Majesty's**
**Prison** ◆ **Cee's Super**
**Store**

Church Folley

*Victoria*

**Columbus Landfall** ◆ **Victoria**
**National Park** **Library**

*Hall's*

**Plaza** ◆ *Salina*

**Post Office** ◆

*Barrack St.*

**Turks & Caicos Bank** ◆ Mission Folley

*Murphy's Alley* 1

**Lime Wireless** ◆

*Pond St.*

Talbot Folley

*Duke St.*

◆ **Courthouse** Moxie Folley

2

Good St.

2 3

Osborne Road

4 3

*James St.*

Barracks Hill Rd.

Closehall Rd.

*Salina*

4 *Salina*

**Holy Cross** ◆
**Catholic Church**

Airport Road

### KEY
**1** *Restaurants*
1 *Hotels*
*i* *Tourist Information*

TO AIRPORT AND
CRUISE SHIP PORT
↓

### Restaurants
Birdcage Restaurant, **4**
Mookie Pookie Pizza
Palace, **1**
Sand Bar, **2**
Secret Garden, **3**

### Hotels
Crabtree Apartments, **4**
Grand Turk Inn
Bed & Breakfast, **1**
Osprey Beach Hotel, **3**
Salt Raker Inn, **2**

lunchtime, the tiny eatery is packed with locals ordering specials such as steamed beef, curried chicken, and curried goat. You can also get burgers and omelets, but stick to the specials if you want fast service, and dine in if you want to get a true taste of island living. By night, the place becomes Grand Turk's only take-out pizza place. $ *Average main: $12* ✉ *Hospital Rd., Cockburn Town* ▭ *No credit cards* ⊘ *Closed Sun.*

**$$** ✕ **Sand Bar.** *American.* Run by two Canadian sisters, this popular beachside bar is a good value; the menu is limited to fish-and-chips, quesadillas, and similarly basic bar fare. The tented wooden terrace jutting out onto the beach provides shade during the day, making it an ideal lunch spot, but it's also a great place to watch the sunset. The service is friendly, and the local crowd often spills into the street. $ *Average main: $14* ✉ *Duke St., Cockburn Town.*

**$$** ✕ **Secret Garden.** *Seafood.* Simply prepared garlic shrimp or grilled grouper are among the more popular dishes at this local favorite. Located behind Salt Raker Inn in a pretty courtyard garden, it more than lives up to its name. Friday nights feature live music by rake-and-scrape bands. $ *Average main: $17* ✉ *Cockburn Town* ☎ *649/946–2260.*

**GRAND TURK LIVE.** Want to know what the weather is like on Grand Turk? Now you can check it 24 hours a day at ⊕ www.grand-turkcc.com, the website for the Grand Turk Cruise Center. You can also check to see if there's a ship in port.

## PILLORY BEACH

**$$$** ✕ **Guanahani Restaurant and Bar.** *International.* Off the town's main drag, this restaurant sits on a stunning but quiet stretch of beach. The food goes beyond the usual Grand Turk fare and is some of the best in town, thanks to the talents of executive chef Jorika Mhende, who takes care of the evening meals. The menu changes daily, based partly on the fresh fish catch. Thursday nights feature a different country's cuisine every time, so sauces and spices are based on that pick. $ *Average main: $26* ✉ *Bohio Dive Resort & Spa, Pillory Beach* ☎ *649/946–2135* ⊕ *www. bohioresort.com.*

## GRAND TURK CRUISE TERMINAL

$$ ✕**Capt Hook's Grill.** *American.* A location next to the cruise port puts you close to the hub but far enough away to relax. Grilled sandwiches with tropical coleslaw are served under a huge gazebo facing the beach. The food is casual and great. Service can be slow, but in a place like this it's not a bad thing—you'll just have more time to admire the view, although it can get loud here when a ship is parked. Hours can vary, so call ahead. $ *Average main: $12* ⊠ *White Sands Beach Resort, next to the cruise port, Grand Turk Cruise Terminal* ☎ *649/946–2991* ⊘ *Closed Sun.*

$ ✕**Jack's Shack.** *American.* Walk 500 meters down the beach from the cruise terminal and you'll find this local beach bar. It gets busy with volleyball players, and offers chair rentals and tropical drinks. Casual food such as burgers and hot dogs satisfy your hunger. Print a coupon from the website for a free shot of T&C's local rum, Bamberra. $ *Average main: $12* ⊠ *North of the pier, Grand Turk Cruise Terminal* ☎ *649/232–0099* ⊘ *Closed any time a ship is not in port.*

$$ ✕**Jimmy Buffet's Margaritaville.** *American.* When you're at this branch of the party-loving chain restaurant, you can engage in cruise activities even though you're on land. One of the largest Margaritavilles in the world opens its doors when a cruise ship is parked at the dock. Tables are scattered around a large winding pool; there's even a DJ and a FlowRider (a wave pool where you can surf on land—for a fee). You can enjoy 52 flavors of margaritas or the restaurant's own beer, Landshark, while you eat casual bar food such as wings, quesadillas, and burgers. The food is good, the people-watching is great. $ *Average main: $15* ⊠ *Grand Turk Cruise Terminal* ☎ *649/946–1880* ⊕ *www. margaritavillecaribbean.com* ⊘ *Closed when no cruise ships are at the pier.*

# Of Hurricanes and Wild Weater

Since 1984, when the increase in tourism began here, the Turks and Caicos have largely escaped the wrath of hurricanes and tropical storms that have battered the nearby Bahamas regularly. As one of the driest island chains in the southern Atlantic, they rarely even get much rainfall.

Even during a rare and much-needed downpour, you may see rain on one part of Provo but not a drop on the other side of the island. When a weather report says there is a 30% to 60% chance of rain, you can usually assume that only *one* of the islands in the archipelago might get a rain shower but not the others. There could be rain on North Caicos, for example, but not even a cloud in the skies over Provo. Sometimes you will see rain even as the sun is shining on you! These sun showers only last a couple of minutes. An hour of rain is often followed by an hour of bright sunlight.

A major hurricane had not hit the Turks and Caicos directly for more than 50 years. But in September 2008 the islands received a double whammy: back-to-back hurricanes—Hurricane Hanna and Hurricane Ike—and just a week apart. During Hanna, a Category 1 storm, the hurricane's eye passed over Provo an unusual three times; the storm then remained stationary over the island for almost four full days, dumping water 24 hours a day. No one had prepared for Hanna, because forecasts had not shown it passing anywhere close to Provo.

Less than a week later Hurricane Ike—a Category 4 storm—passed through the island chain. Most buildings on Provo lost roof shingles and basic landscaping, but the island bounced back fairly quickly.

On Grand Turk, Salt Cay, and South Caicos it was a different story entirely. There was so much destruction and disarray that it took months just to restore power to the islands. Construction companies from Provo sent workers over quickly to help restore the harder-hit islands, and the cruise lines that call in Grand Turk also sent help. In fact, the cruise stops resumed about a month later. In 2011, Hurricane Irene hit Turks and Caicos as a Category 2, but this time everyone was prepared, and the storm caused no major damage.

Everything is now up and running, as if these storms never happened. If you are traveling during hurricane season, it's always wise to get travel insurance, even if a major hurricane strike takes another 50 years.

# WHERE TO STAY

Accommodations include original Bermudian inns, more modern but small beachfront hotels, and basic to well-equipped self-catering suites and apartments. Almost all hotels offer dive packages, which are an excellent value.

*For expanded hotel reviews, visit Fodors.com.*

## COCKBURN TOWN

$   ⊞ **Crabtree Apartments.** *Rental.* On their own secluded stretch of beach, these three apartments make a quiet getaway that is far enough from the cruise-ship port to give you some peace and quiet, but still within walking distance of Duke and Front streets. **Pros:** private beachfront; the art on the walls adds a tropical touch. **Cons:** hard to find; a longer walk to restaurants than from hotels closer to town; five-night minimum makes it hard to use as a base for a quick trip from Provo. Ⓢ *Rooms from: $250* ⊠ *Close Hall Rd., Cockburn Town* ☎ *649/468–2410, 978/270–1698* ⊕ *www.grandturkvacationrental.com* ⇨ *3 2-bedroom apartments* ⓞ *No meals* ⌖ *5-night minimum.*

$$   ⊞ **Grand Turk Inn Bed & Breakfast.** *B&B/Inn.* Staying at this true B&B, one of just a few in all the Turks and Caicos, gives you a feel for the way the Caribbean used to be, without requiring you to give up comfort. **Pros:** charming old Caribbean clapboard house; faces the beach; all guests lent a local cell phone. **Cons:** no kids under 16. Ⓢ *Rooms from: $300* ⊠ *Front St., Cockburn Town* ☎ *649/333–7791* ⊕ *www.grandturkinn.com* ⇨ *5 rooms* ⓞ *Breakfast.*

★   **Fodor's**Choice ⊞ **Osprey Beach Hotel.** *Hotel.* The veteran hote-
$   lier Jenny Smith has transformed this two-story ocean-front hotel with artistic touches: palms, frangipani, and deep-green azaleas frame it like a painting. **Pros:** best hotel on Grand Turk; walking distance to Front Street, restaurants, and excursions. **Cons:** three-night minimum; rocky beachfront. Ⓢ *Rooms from: $225* ⊠ *Duke St., Cockburn Town* ☎ *649/946–2666* ⊕ *www.ospreybeachhotel.com* ⇨ *11 rooms, 16 suites* ⓞ *No meals* ⌖ *3-night minimum.*

$   ⊞ **Salt Raker Inn.** *B&B/Inn.* A large anchor on the sun-dappled pathway marks the entrance to this 19th-century house, which is now an unpretentious inn. **Pros:** excellent location that is an easy walk to Front Street, restaurants, and excursions. **Cons:** the lack of no-smoking rooms. Ⓢ *Rooms from: $115* ⊠ *Duke St., Cockburn Town* ☎ *649/946–2260* ⊕ *www.hotelsaltraker.com* ⇨ *10 rooms, 3 suites* ⓞ *No meals.*

## PILLORY BEACH

**$** ☷ **Bohio Dive Resort and Spa.** *Resort.* Divers are all drawn to this basic yet comfortable hotel. **Pros:** Guanahani is probably the best restaurant in Grand Turk; on a gorgeous beach; steps away from awesome snorkeling. **Cons:** three-night minimum doesn't allow for quick getaways from Provo. Ⓢ *Rooms from: $195* ✉ *Pillory Beach* ☎ *649/946–2135* ⊕ *www.bohioresort. com* ⤳ *12 rooms, 4 suites* ⦿ *No meals* ☞ *3-night minimum.*

## GRAND TURK CRUISE TERMINAL

**$** ☷ **White Sands Beach Resort.** *Rental.* Though these condos are next to the cruise-ship port with its daily action, you're still on a quiet stretch of beach made just for relaxing. **Pros:** on a beautiful stretch of beach; gazebo is great for watching the sunset; resort will help set up dive packages with local operators. **Cons:** far enough from the main hub that you need a car or taxi. Ⓢ *Rooms from: $150* ✉ *Next to cruise teriminal, Grand Turk Cruise Terminal* ☎ *649/946–1065* ⊕ *www.whitesandstci.com* ⤳ *16 apartments* ⦿ *No meals.*

# SPORTS AND THE OUTDOORS

## ADVENTURE TOURS

**Chukka Caribbean Adventures.** Chukka Caribbean Adventures, the Jamaica-based adventure-tour operator, runs most of the cruise excursions on Grand Turk, but you don't have to be on a cruise ship to take part in the fun. Even if you are staying at a hotel on Grand Turk, you can still sign up for activities, even if there is no cruise ship moored at the Grand Turk Cruise Terminal. You can join a group horseback ride and swim, dune-buggy safari, or 4x4 safari. In fact, staying on land may offer you an advantage. If you're staying more than a couple of days on the island, you can enjoy them all and not have to limit yourself because of ship time constraints. Be sure to call ahead for availability. ✉ *Grand Turk Cruise Terminal* ☎ *649/332–1339* ⊕ *www.ChukkaCaribbean.com.*

## CYCLING

If you love to ride a bike, then out of all of the islands in Turks and Caicos, Grand Turk is your island because it's both small enough and flat enough that it's possible to tour it by bike. You will find biking the perfect (and for some preferred) mode of transportation for people living here. The island's mostly flat terrain isn't very taxing, and

# Grand Turk in a Day

It's easy to take a day trip from Provo to Grand Turk, to see this sleepy colorful island that's completely different from Provo. Make arrangements before going over so that you can have a golf cart, bike, or car waiting at the airport.

From the airport take a right and drive to Front Street. Walk the colorful quiet street with historical houses. Do not miss the small Turks & Caicos National Museum—even if you are not a museum person—as this one is quite fascinating. If a cruise ship is at port, then you can tour Her Majesty's Jail. Stop at Bohio Dive Resort, north past Front Street (take your transportation), and have lunch. You can also snorkel here and enjoy Pillory Beach.

If there's a cruise ship at port, you can also go out and see the lighthouse. It only takes 10 minutes to get there.

Also, if a cruise ship is at port, you can go past the airport to the cruise port to check out the shopping there and people-watch. The stores at the cruise terminal are the only real shops on island, and there's also a casino. It's a complete contrast to Front Street.

If no cruise ship is at port, set up an excursion to Gibbs Cay to swim with stingrays, skipping the lighthouse, prison museum, and cruise terminal shopping. You'll need to be back at the airport 30 minutes before the flight back to Provo.

4

most roads have hard surfaces. Take water with you: there are few places to stop for refreshments. Most hotels have bicycles available, but you can also rent them for $10 to $15 a day from Oasis Divers (*see ⇨ Diving and Snorkeling*), which also offers fun Segway tours.

## DIVING AND SNORKELING

In these waters you can find undersea cathedrals, coral gardens, and countless tunnels, but note that you must carry and present a valid certificate card before you'll be allowed to dive. As its name suggests, the Black Forest offers staggering black-coral formations as well as the occasional black-tip shark. In the Library you can study fish galore, including large numbers of yellowtail snapper. At the Columbus Passage separating South Caicos from Grand Turk, each side of a 22-mile-wide (35-km-wide) channel drops more than 7,000 feet. From January through March thousands of Atlantic humpback whales swim through

## CLOSE UP — Cruise Activities for Island Visitors

Grand Turk is a unique destination in that there are places on the island that are only open when there is a cruise ship at the port; the good news is that you don't need to be on a cruise to enjoy most of these sights and activities.

For visitors to Grand Turk, the trick is to visit these places as soon as a ship pulls up but before the passengers have a chance to disembark; because disembarkation on a large ship can take a half hour or more under the best circumstances, you'll have plenty of time to enjoy some of these sights when they first open but before the cruise crowds arrive. The lighthouse and the old prison are two possibilities.

The shops at the cruise port are only open when there is a ship in port, and vendors will line Front Street when a ship arrives, so go then if you want to shop.

Some other activities are only offered on cruise days, including ATV tours and guided, off-road dirt-bike rides. So if you happen to be on Grand Turk on a cruise-ship day, take full advantage of everything it has to offer.

---

en route to their winter breeding grounds. Gibb's Cay, a small cay a couple of miles off Grand Turk, makes a great excursion for swimming with stingrays.

Dive outfitters can all be found in Cockburn Town. Two-tank boat dives generally cost $60 to $80.

**Blue Water Divers.** In operation on Grand Turk since 1983, Blue Water Divers is the only PADI Gold Palm five-star dive center on the island. The owner, Mitch, may put some of your underwater adventures to music in the evenings when he plays at the Osprey Beach Hotel or Salt Raker Inn. ⊠ *Duke St., Cockburn Town* ☎ *649/946–2432* ⊕ *www.grandturkscuba.com.*

**Grand Turk Diving.** The outfitter offers full-service dives and trips to Gibbs Cay and Salt Cay. ⊠ *Cockburn Town* ☎ *649/946–1559* ⊕ *www.gtdiving.com.*

 **Oasis Divers.** Oasis Divers provides complete gear handling and pampering treatment. It also supplies Nitrox and rebreathers. The company also offers a wide variety of other tours, as well as renting bicycles and operating Segway tours. ⊠ *Duke St., Cockburn Town* ☎ *649/946–1128* ⊕ *www.oasisdivers.com.*

WORD OF MOUTH. "Grand Turk had some of the best snorkeling and diving in the West Indies. Right up there with Belize and Andros. With a 7,000 foot wall just 50 yards off the beach on the west side of the island, plenty of reefs, and a healthy environment, snorkeling and diving were very vibrant."—Callaloo

# SHOPPING

Shopping in Grand Turk is hard to come by—choices are slim. Let's just say that no true shopaholic would want to come here for vacation. You can get the usual T-shirts and dive trinkets at all the dive shops, but there are only a few options for more interesting shopping opportunities. When a ship is in port, the shops at the pier will be open, and these increase your options dramatically.

## COCKBURN TOWN

**Shop at Grand Turk Inn.** Beautiful place mats and clothing with tropical prints are sold at this B&B. ⊠ *Cockburn Town* ☏ *649/333–7791.*

## PILLORY BEACH

**OceanScapes Spa.** A real spa has finally come to Grand Turk. There are two branches, one at Bohio Dive Resort and another at White Sands Beach Resort. The latter offers treatments outside under a thatched-roof tea hut, which definitely gives the spa tropical flair. Massages are $20 per 15 minutes. ⊠ *Bohio Dive Resort, Pillory Beach* ☏ *649/232–6201* ⊕ *oceanscapesspa.com.*

## GRAND TURK CRUISE TERMINAL

**The Goldsmith.** The Goldsmith, part of a Turks and Caicos chain, has the island's largest selection of jewelry, as well as clothing, cigars, and lots more. ⊠ *Grand Turk Cruise Terminal.*

**Piranha Joe's.** The T-shirts and jackets here all have "Grand Turk" printed on them. ⊠ *Grand Turk Cruise Terminal.*

**Ron Jon Surf Shop.** The Ron Jon Surf Shop sells bathing suits, T-shirts, bumper stickers, and beer mugs with its famous logo on them. ⊠ *Grand Turk Cruise Terminal* ⊕ *www.ronjons.com.*

# NIGHTLIFE

Grand Turk is a quiet place, where you come to relax and unwind, so most of the nightlife consists of little more than a happy hour at sunset so you have a chance to glimpse the elusive green flash. Most restaurants turn into gathering places where you can talk with the new friends you have made that day, but there a few more nightlife-oriented places that will keep you busy after dark.

**Osprey Beach Hotel.** Every Wednesday and Sunday, there's lively rake-and-scrape music at the Osprey Beach Hotel. ✉ *Duke St., Cockburn Town* ☎ *649/946–2666.*

**Salt Raker Inn.** On Friday, rake-and-scrape bands play at the Salt Raker Inn. ✉ *Duke St., Cockburn Town* ☎ *649/946– 2260* ⊕ *www.saltrakerinn.com.*

**Santa Maria Gaming Saloon.** You don't have to leave the beach to gamble on Grand Turk. This casino has been built to look like a pirate ship and is at White Sands Beach Resort near the cruise terminal. You can try your luck at more than 100 slots, state-of-the-art poker machines, roulette, and blackjack. There's also an outdoor upstairs deck to enjoy the great outdoors with live bands when a ship is in port. ✉ *White Sands Resort, Grand Turk Cruise Terminal* ☎ *649/242–5758* ⊕ *www.santamariacasino.com.*

RAKE-AND-SCRAPE. The official music of Turks and Caicos is called rake-and-scrape (or often "rake 'n' scrape"); it's sometimes also known as ripsaw music. It's reputed to have started on tiny Cat Island in the Bahamas. The music is made using goombay drums, carved out of steel-container drums used during shipping. Other "instruments" are added using tools, especially a carpenter's saw, or whatever is on hand. Its inspiration is the music of Africa, and it is particularly popular on more isolated islands. You can still find rake-and-scrape bands around the islands, but they are more prevalent on Grand Turk and South Caicos.

# SALT CAY

By
Ramona
Settle

**IN THE 19TH CENTURY THE SALINAS** of Salt Cay produced much of the world's supply of salt. More than 1,000 people lived on the island then, most employed in the salt industry, at a time when salt was as valuable as gold. When the salt trade dried up, nearly everyone moved on to other islands. Today, there are only about 180 inhabitants. Chances are you will meet quite a few of them by the end of your stay, whether you're here for one day or many.

As you approach Salt Cay, either by boat or by plane, you may wonder what you've gotten yourself into. The land is dry and brown, the island seems too small to occupy you for even a day trip. Don't worry. Salt Cay has a way of getting into your blood and leaving a lasting impression. By the end of your first day you may very well be plotting a return trip.

# PLANNING

## PLANNING YOUR TIME

As an island of only 2½ square miles (6 square km), Salt Cay is so small that you can practically walk around it and soak up its charms in a couple of hours, but you'll have more fun if you take your time, ideally spending at least one night on the island. Start at Porter's Island Thyme Bistro, whose owner, Porter Williams, is the know-all of Salt Cay. He will provide an orientation package, information about island activities, and if you wish, a box lunch to take to the scenic coastline—where there's whale-watching in season. Try to find pirate graves and visit some of the off-the-beaten-path spots on beautiful North Beach. If you dive, make an appointment with Debbie of Salt Cay Divers to show you the wrecks. Or book a whale-watching or shark-viewing trip with Crystal Seas Adventures, whose owner Tim Dunn possesses a remarkable knowledge of these waters. Be sure to drive past the abandoned Governor's Mansion. You'll notice that the walls around each home have embedded conch shells to keep out the donkeys and cows—you'll find yourself stopping frequently for the friendly donkeys, who rule the roads. End your night listening to live music at Coral Reef Bar and Grill or Bingo Night at Porter's Island Thyme. If it's pizza night, head back to Porter's Island Thyme Bistro; Porter makes great pizza. If Salt Cay lacks natural beauty, it definitely does not lack character (or is it that it has characters?). By the end of your stay, you will have made some lifelong friends.

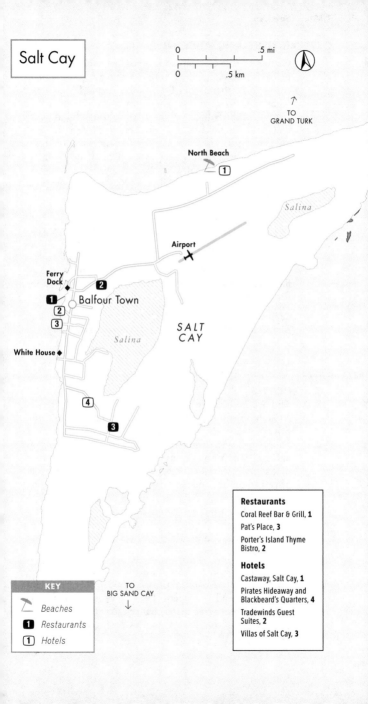

## GETTING HERE AND AROUND

Getting to Salt Cay can sometimes feel like an adventure in itself. Although Grand Turk is a skip away, it's actually easier to get here from Provo on a regularly scheduled flight on Caicos Express. There is twice-weekly ferry from Grand Turk to Salt Cay (weather permitting). But if you're on Grand Turk and want to travel before the ferry is scheduled, ask at the dive shops to see if someone can take you over in a private boat. To get back to Grand Turk from Salt Cay, ask Debbie at Salt Cay Divers. The 30- to 40-minute boat trip typically costs $250 to $300, but the weather can sometimes put a damper on your travel plans.

Once you reach Salt Cay, you can rent a golf cart from Candy at Pirate's Hideaway. A rented golf cart is a fun way to get out and explore on your own. There's only one named street here, so getting around is easy—and anyone you meet can give you directions. Driving through the salt flats to North Beach is an adventure in itself, and stopping for donkeys to cross the road adds to the charm.

**Contacts Caicos Express** ☎ 649/243–0237 ⊕ *caicosexpressairways. com.* **Salt Cay Airport** (*SLX*). ☎ 649/496–4999. **Salt Cay Ferry** ☎ 649/244–1407 ⊕ *www.turksandcaicoswhalewatching.com.*

## ESSENTIALS

### HOTELS

The accommodations in Salt Cay are basic, with just enough amenities to keep you comfortable. You'll find private villas, apartments, and a couple of small guesthouse-style accommodations. Most visitors who come to Salt Cay won't mind a little rusticity; the island attracts that type of traveler. Come here to enjoy the Caribbean of yesteryear and to enjoy nature. You won't be roughing it—while most places count on sea breezes for cooling, you'll still find the occasional air-conditioner, as well as satellite TV and Wi-Fi. What you do get in every one of our recommended lodgings are pleasant hosts who welcome you like family.

### RESTAURANTS

There are only a handful of restaurants on Salt Cay, but food is generally excellent. Pat's Place is a home-based restaurant, where the menu changes according to what the boats bring in that day. At night Coral Reef Bar & Grill

## TOP REASONS TO GO

**Beaches.** Bar none, North Beach is the best on Salt Cay. Although getting to the beach is not easy, the beach itself is 3 miles (5 km) of pure bliss, with bright white sand, absolutely no rocks or seaweed, glowing neon-blue water, and views of Grand Turk. It's usually deserted, and offers the island's best opportunities for off-beach snorkeling and whale-watching.

**Clamming and pirates.** Have your kids collect clams in the shallows for an experience they won't soon forget. It's fun for adults, too. Candy from Pirate's Hideaway will help you search. When you're done clamming, head down Victoria Street in search of pirate graves (sometimes marked only by a pile of stones).

**Hanging with the locals.** Since the island has a population of about 180, chances are pretty good you will meet a decent percentage of them during your visit. Don't be surprised if someone steps out to greet you on your explorations. Soon you'll be moving between Coral Reef Bar & Grill and Porter's Island Thyme Bistro, and you'll meet everyone there is to meet.

**Whale-Watching.** Take an excursion for your chance to actually swim with whales in season from mid-January to mid-April. Explore Sand Cay, which has the most neon turquoise you'll see. In summer months sharks breed here, too.

**Doing absolutely nothing.** The best days on Salt Cay are those when you do nothing at all. You can sleep in, read a book, walk around, have a lazy lunch, take a nap, snorkel a little, bird-watch, take pictures, take another nap, feed the donkeys, go beachcombing, maybe take another nap. You may be so busy doing nothing that you'll forget to check your email.

and Porter's Island Thyme Bistro turn into lively night-spots, and you're likely to see virtually everyone you meet during the day at one or the other. Reservations for dinner are essential everywhere; the cooks have to plan ahead, so if you just show up you may not be fed.

# EXPLORING SALT CAY

Salt sheds and salinas are silent reminders of the days when the island was a leading producer of salt. Now the salt ponds attract abundant birdlife. Island tours are often conducted by motorized golf cart. From January through April, humpback whales pass by on the way to their winter breeding grounds.

What little development there is on Salt Cay is found in Balfour Town. It's home to several small hotels and a few cozy stores, as well as the main dock and the Coral Reef Bar & Grill, where locals hang out with tourists to watch the sunset and drink a beer.

**White House.** This grand stone house, which once belonged to a wealthy salt merchant, is testimony to the heyday of Salt Cay's eponymous industry. Still owned by the descendants of the original family, it's sometimes opened up for tours. Ask Tim Dunn, a descendant of the original owners, as he may give you a personal tour to see the still-intact, original furnishings, books, and medicine cabinet that date back to the early 1800s. ✉ *Victoria St., Balfour Town* 🖅 *Free* ⊘ *By appointment only.*

WORD OF MOUTH. "The snorkeling [on Salt Cay] is unbelievable, and the beaches are all different. North Beach has some of the most beautiful beaches I have ever seen!"—Caryn_Hersh

# BEACHES

**North Beach.** North Beach is the best reason to visit Salt Cay; it might be the finest beach in the Turks and Caicos, if not the world. Part of the beauty lies not just in the soft, powdery sand and bright blue water but in its isolation; it's very likely that you will have this lovely beach all to yourself. **Amenities:** none. **Best for:** solitude; snorkeling; swimming; walking.

**Big Sand Cay.** Accessible by boat with the on-island tour operators, Big Sand Cay, 7 miles (11 km) south of Salt Cay, is tiny and totally uninhabited; it's also known for its long, unspoiled stretches of open sand. **Amenities:** none. **Best for:** swimming. ✉ *7 miles (11 km) south of the island.*

CLOSE UP

## The Versatile Islander

On an island this small almost every local must be a jack-of-all-trades. Because everything has to be imported and flown in (even the people); you will find that locals have become very resourceful. Chances are the singer in the band you are listening to during dinner was also your dive master earlier in the day. Your tour guide might be the hotel's electrician. The cab driver you meet on arrival at the airport might also be your boat captain on an excursion later in the day, and the check-in clerk at the airport counter might sell you the jewelry she makes at one of the little beachside shops. After a day or two, you will start recognizing people everywhere from all the different things they can do.

5

# WHERE TO EAT

Although small in size, the three restaurants on Salt Cay serve food that's big in flavor, with some of the best food in the islands.

**$$** ✕**Coral Reef Bar and Grill.** *Caribbean.* This small restaurant sits on a beachside deck. It's colorfully painted in red, yellow, and sky-blue, and the people who hang out here are just as colorful. Have a grilled hamburger or the catch of the day, and you'll get to know the locals. The restaurant offers free Wi-Fi so you can check your email while you whale-watch and eat. On most Sundays the island turns out for rib night here. In the evening you can drink beer while listening to a local dive master play guitar and sing. ⑤ *Average main: $15* ✉ *Victoria St., Balfour Town* ☎ *649/241–1009* ⚑ *Reservations essential.*

**$$$** ✕**Pat's Place.** *Caribbean.* Island native Pat Simmons can give you a lesson in the medicinal qualities of her garden plants and periwinkle flowers, as well as provide excellent native cuisine for a very reasonable price in her comforting Salt Cay home. Home cooking doesn't get any closer to home than this. Try conch fritters for lunch and steamed grouper with okra rice for dinner. Pat also has a small grocery shop selling staples. As with all places to eat in Salt Cay, put in your food order in the morning and tell them what time you want to eat. Pat only cooks when there's someone to cook for. ⑤ *Average main: $25* ✉ *South District* ☎ *649/946–6919* ⚑ *Reservations essential* ▭ *No credit cards.*

## The People You Must Meet on Salt Cay

With such a small population, it would be a disservice to not only meet the islanders but mingle with them, too. Make a point to hang out with Porter and his wife Haidee of Porter's Island Thyme Bistro. They know everything about Salt Cay and can reach anyone on island for you. Debbie of Salt Cay Divers remembers everyone's face, and she can help make arrangements for everything from getting there to food staples.

Tim of Crystal Sea Adventures lives at the White House, which was built by his ancestors. If you're lucky, he might give you a tour of this majestic, historic home. Last but not least, there's Candy of Pirates Hideaway. She is artistic and colorful, and there's no one who knows the history of these islands like she does. Do not leave Salt Cay without meeting these individuals; they will be your friends for life.

★ Fodor's Choice ✕ **Porter's Island Thyme Bistro.** *Eclectic.* Owner
**$$$** Porter Williams serves potent alcoholic creations as well as fairly sophisticated local and international cuisine. Try steamed, freshly caught snapper in a pepper-wine sauce with peas and rice, or spicy-hot chicken curry served with tangy chutneys. Or you can order the "Porter" house steak. You can take cooking lessons from the chef, enjoy the nightly Filipino fusion tapas during happy hour, and join the gang for Friday-night pizza. This is a great place to make friends and the best place to catch up on island gossip. The airy, trellis-covered spot overlooks the salinas. There's a small shop with gifts and tourist information; you can also get a manicure or pedicure here. Reservations are essential here; put in your order for food in the morning and tell Porter what time you want to eat. Then explore; food will be waiting for you. ⑤ *Average main: $26* ✉ *Balfour Town* ☎ *649/946–6977* ⊕ *www.islandthyme.tc* ⌛ *Reservations essential* ⊗ *Closed Wed. mid-May–June and Sept.–late Oct.*

# WHERE TO STAY

Salt Cay has a handful of small inns and apartment-style lodgings, but the majority of people stay in house rentals.

*For expanded hotel reviews, visit Fodors.com.*

## HOUSE AND VILLA RENTALS

Salt Cay has no full-service hotels or resorts, but there are many small homes to rent on the island, and many visitors go this route instead of staying in one of the handful of small inns or B&Bs. A typical Salt Cay villa is **Purple Conch Cottage** (⊕ *Purpleconch.com*, 2 beds/1 bath, $125 nightly), which is independently owned and managed by the owners. Most rental villas are like this one, basic and rustic, yet charming.

Three main property managers on island oversee the rental of almost all of these vacation homes, and they can also help you set up tours, take you sightseeing, and troubleshoot anything that goes wrong during your stay (or pick you up and drive you to a restaurant).

**Candy Herwin.** Candy Herwin of Pirates Hideaway oversees the nicest place to stay on the island, Brown House (*Saltcaywaterfront.com*, $659 nightly for 3 bedrooms), an original plantation home from the salt-raking era that has ocean views and has been lovingly restored. Candy can also regale you with stories about the history of Salt Cay, which will enhance your stay. ☎ *649/244–1407* ⊕ *www.Saltcay.tc.*

**Debbie Manos.** Along with Trade Winds Guest Suites, Debbie Manos of Salt Cay Divers manages the Charming House (*Charleslaurence.com*, $114 nightly), an original salt-raker home in the historic quarter across from Governor's House. ☎ *649/241–1009* ⊕ *www.saltcaydivers.tc.*

**Porter Williams.** Along with the Castaway apartment rentals on North Beach, Porter Williams, who owns Porter's Island Thyme, also oversees some additional private villas that have a great beachy feel and are extremely affordable. These include Twilight Zone, a small one-bedroom home ($110 per night) with a walk to the beach, and Salt Cay Beach House, which actually consists of twin side-by-side cottages facing the ocean that rent for $130 a night. ☎ *649/946–6977* ⊕ *www.islandthyme.tc.*

## RECOMMENDED LODGINGS

★ Fodor'sChoice ☒ **Castaway, Salt Cay.** *Rental.* This only lodg-
$$$ ing that sits directly on the stunning 3-mile (5-km) North
Beach might just be what the doctor ordered if you're in
need of total relaxation—it can be hard to fathom having
one of the world's most beautiful beaches all to yourself.
**Pros:** on a spectacular beach; truly a get away from it
all; perfect for relaxing. **Cons:** it's a dark, secluded road
into town at night. ⑤*Rooms from: $285* ☒*North Beach*
☎*649/946–6977* ⊕*www.castawayonsaltcay.com* ⌑*4 suites*
☉*Multiple meal plans.*

$$ ☒ **Pirates Hideaway and Blackbeard's Quarters.** *Rental.* Owner
Candy Herwin—true to her self-proclaimed pirate status—
has smuggled artistic treasures across the ocean and created
her own masterpieces to deck out this lair. **Pros:** island
personality throughout; great snorkling off the beachfront. **Cons:** the closest swimming beach a five-minute
walk. ⑤*Rooms from: $175* ☒*Victoria St., Balfour Town*
☎*649/946–6909* ⊕*www.saltcay.tc* ⌑*3 suites, 1 cottage*
☉*No meals.*

$$ ☒ **Tradewinds Guest Suites.** *Rental.* A grove of whispering
casuarina trees surrounds these five single-story, basic apart-
ments, which offer a moderate-budget option on Salt Cay
with the option of dive packages. **Pros:** walking distance to
diving, fishing, dining. **Cons:** air-conditioning costs extra;
too isolated for some people. ⑤*Rooms from: $161* ☒*Victo-
ria St., Balfour Town* ☎*649/946–6906* ⊕*www.tradewinds.
tc* ⌑*5 apartments* ☉*No meals.*

$$ ☒ **Villas of Salt Cay.** *Rental.* One of the most convenient
places to stay in Salt Cay is centrally located on Victoria
Street, in the middle of everything. **Pros:** bedrooms are
set up for extra privacy; on Victoria Street within walking distance of everything; on a private stretch of beach.
**Cons:** not all rooms have air-conditioning; cabanas don't
have kitchens; shared pool. ⑤*Rooms from: $225* ☒*Victoria
St., Balfour Town* ☎*649/343–2157* ⊕*www.villasofsaltcay.
tc* ⌑*1 2-bedroom villa, 1 1-bedroom cottage, 3 cabanas*
☉*No meals.*

# SPORTS AND THE OUTDOORS

## DIVING AND SNORKELING

Scuba divers can explore the wreck of the *Endymion,* a 140-foot wooden-hull British warship that sank in 1790; you can swim through the hull and spot cannons and anchors. It's off the southern point of Salt Cay.

**Salt Cay Divers.** Salt Cay Divers conducts daily dive trips and rents out all the necessary equipment. In season, they run whale-watching trips. They can also help get you to Salt Cay from Provo or Grand Turk, and stock your villa with groceries. ☎ *649/946–6906* ⊕ *www.saltcaydivers.tc.*

## WHALE-WATCHING

During the winter months (January through April), Salt Cay is a center for whale-watching, when some 2,500 humpback whales pass close to shore. Whale-watching trips can be organized with Crystal Seas Adventures. Tim knows how to spot those whales and get you close to them.

★ Fodors Choice **Crystal Seas Adventures.** Proprietor Tim Dunn, whose family descends from the original owners of Salt Cay's historic White House, knows these waters as well as anybody. His company offers a variety of excursions: diving with stingrays at Gibbs Cay, and trips to Grand Turk and secluded beaches, such as Great Sand Cay. Whale-watching is also very popular, and Dunn is the only outfitter with diving trips to South Caicos, reputed to be one of the best places in the world for this. ☎ *649/243–9843* ⊕ *www.crystalseasadventures.com.*

**Salt Cay Adventure Tours.** Whale-watching tours are available for two or more hours. They also offer a biweekly round-trip ferry to Grand Turk. Fish with local fishermen, boat ride to National Museum on Grand Turk, or take a tour of historic Salt Cay's landmarks. ✉ *South District* ☎ *649/244–1407* ⊕ *www.saltcaytours.com.*

## SHOPPING

There was a time when the only choice for visitors was to rent a boat and head to Grand Turk for basic food supplies and sundries (or have your self-catering accommodations provide provisioning for you). Now it is easier to be self-sufficient in Salt Cay. Nettie's Grocery Store not only bakes fresh bread but also offers basic food supplies. Pat's Place now has two small shops, one with basic groceries and one with sundries. Elouisa's also offers some basic groceries. Ask anyone on the island where to find these small shops; the streets have no names, but it's easy to walk around the few blocks of town to find them. However, if there is anything you can't live without, the best advice is to bring it with you from home or make a grocery run in Provo and carry the food with you to Salt Cay.

For souvenirs, Salt Cay Divers has a small boutique with art prints and clothes and jewelry. The best place to buy arts and crafts is at Porter's Island Thyme Bistro; the ceiling planks are decorated with original Haitian oils that can be purchased, and Porter also sells art prints, including one of Porter's Island Thyme by famous Caribbean artist Shari Erikson. Porter also sells jewelry, T-shirts of Porter's Island Thyme, and hanging, decorative, colorful fish.

**Salt Cay Salt Works.** In it's heyday, Salt Cay was one of the richest islands in the world because of its salt. Now Haidee, the wife of Porter Williams (of Porter's Island Thyme Bistro), lovingly prepares the native salt in colored bottles in different forms to purchase as a keepsake (or to use on margaritas!). You can buy it in Porter's Island Thyme's shop. ⊠ *Porter's Island Thyme Bistro, Balfour Town* ☎ *649/946–6977* ⊕ *www.saltcaysaltworks.com.*

# TRAVEL SMART
# TURKS & CAICOS

# GETTING HERE AND AROUND

You arrive on Provo by air, and then you need to rent or take taxis to get around. The island is flat and has no traffic lights; most places are no farther than 20 minutes away. On Grand Turk it's fun to get around by bicycle or scooter; the island is small and the roads are in good condition. On tiny Salt Cay, Parrot Cay, and Pine Cay, the preferred mode of transportation is a golf cart. There's a ferry to North Caicos; the rest of the islands require a boat or plane to reach them, though you can now drive on the causeway from North Caicos to Middle Caicos.

■TIP→ **Ask the local tourist board about hotel packages during the November Conch Festival, when the great restaurants of Provo compete with live music and activities.**

## ▌ AIR TRAVEL

The main gateway into the Turks and Caicos Islands is Providenciales International Airport, though the Grand Turk International Airport can also handle larger jets. For private planes, Provo Air Center is a full-service FBO (Fixed Base Operator) offering refueling, maintenance, and short-term storage, as well as on-site customs and immigration clearance, a lounge, and concierge services. Even if you are going on to other islands in the chain, you will probably stop in Provo first for customs, then take a domestic flight onward.

---

### AIRLINE TIP

If you have an afternoon flight, check in your bags early in the morning (keep a change of clothes in a carry-on), then go back to the beach for one last lunch, returning to the airport an hour before your flight departs. It makes for much easier traveling, saves time, and you get your last beach fix.

---

### AIRPORTS

At this writing, all scheduled international flights to Turks and Caicos Islands arrive in Providenciales, aka Provo, so this is where you will go through immigration and customs. Make sure you have all of your paperwork completely filled out, as immigration lines can be slow; in fact, on a busy day you may wait 30 to 40 minutes from the time you disembark to the time you pass through customs. If you are on a private or chartered plane, you can also go through immigration and customs at Grand Turk. Airlines will tell you to arrive at the airport three hours before your return flight; this is a good advice in most cases because security will inspect all your luggage by hand before allowing you to check in. During the week, two hours is probably enough time, but on Saturday or Sunday—especially during peak season—three hours is more appropriate.

For those in a hurry, Provo's airport offers the VIP Travels Club. For a fee, you get speedy check-in, priority through security, and your own personal waiting room with TV, Wi-Fi, and snacks. It's much nicer than contending with the mobs until the airport expands. The cost is $200 for the first family member, $50 each additional; children under two are free.

**Airport Information Grand Turk International Airport** (*GDT*). ✉ *Grand Turk* ☎ *649/946–2233.* **Pine Cay Airport** (*PIC*) ✉ *Pine Cay* ☎ *No phone.* **Providenciales International Airport** (*PLS*). ✉ *Airport, Providenciales* ☎ *649/941–5670.* **Salt Cay Airport** (*SLX*). ✉ *Salt Cay* ☎ *649/496–4999.* **South Caicos Airport** (*XSC*). ✉ *South Caicos* ☎ *649/946–4999.* **Turks & Caicos Islands Airport Authority.** The TCIAA website has a schedule of all flights coming into and out of the islands, along with real-time delay information. ⊕ *www.tciairports.com.* **VIP Flyers Club** ☎ *649/946–4000* ⊕ *www.vipflyersclub.com.*

## AIRPORT TRANSFERS

In most cases, if you're staying at a hotel or resort there will be a representative holding a sign to greet you when you arrive in Provo; you will then be put into a regular taxi to the resort. (Only a few hotels are allowed to offer real shuttle service; most are required by law to use regular taxis.) Because Amanyara and Parrot Cay are away from the main hub, they are allowed to transport you directly. Even if you have not made prior arrangements, there will be plenty of taxis around to meet each flight.

To the main area of Grace Bay Road, expect to pay around $23 per couple one-way. You can also have a car rental waiting at the airport; all the rental car companies offer this service. If someone is picking you up, they may wait for you in the nearby small parking lot that charges $1 an hour.

On South Caicos and Grand Turk, you should make prior transportation arrangements. On Pine Cay someone will pick you up in a golf cart. On Salt Cay you could walk if need be.

## FLIGHTS

Although carriers and schedules can vary seasonally, there are many nonstop and connecting flights to Providenciales. At this writing, the U.S. nonstop carriers include American (DFW and MIA), United (EWR), Delta (ATL), JetBlue (BOS, JFK), and US Airways (BOS, CLT, PHL); there are flights almost every day, but most airlines do not offer daily flights. There are also flights from other parts of the Caribbean on Air Turks & Caicos; this airline also flies to some of the smaller islands in the chain from Provo. There are also flights from Nassau on Bahamas Air.

**Airline Contacts Air Turks & Caicos** ☎ *649/941–5481* ⊕ *www.airturksandcaicos.com.* **American Airlines** ☎ *649/946–4948, 800/433–7300* ⊕ *www.aa.com.* **Bahamas Air** ☎ *242/377–5505 in Nassau, 800/222–4262* ⊕ *up.bahamasair.com.* **Delta** ☎ *800/241–4141* ⊕ *www.delta.com.* **JetBlue** ☎ *800/538–2583* ⊕ *www.jetblue.*

com. **United Airlines** ☎ *800/864–8331* ⊕ *www.United.com.*
**US Airways** ☎ *800/622–1015* ⊕ *usairways.com.*

### CHARTER FLIGHTS

Caicos Express can fly you from Provo to anywhere that you need to go in the Turks and Caicos (or the Caribbean for that matter). Although the airline has some scheduled flights, most of their work consists of charters. Charters can be expensive because you pay per flight, not by the passenger. However, if your group is going to a smaller island, or wants to combine your trip with other Caribbean islands, it might be the best way to go.

Contacts **Caicos Express** ☎ *649/243–0237* ⊕ *caicosexpressairways.com.*

## ▌ BOAT AND FERRY TRAVEL

Daily scheduled ferry service between Provo and North Caicos is offered by Caribbean Cruisin', with several departures from Walkin Marina in Leeward. There's a twice-weekly ferry from Salt Cay to Grand Turk (weather permitting).

Contacts **Caribbean Cruisin'** ✉ *Walkin Marina, Leeward, Providenciales* ☎ *649/946–5406, 649/231–4191* ⊕ *www.tciferry.com.* **Salt Cay Ferry** ✉ *Salt Cay* ☎ *649/244–1407* ⊕ *www.turksandcaicoswhalewatching.com.*

## ▌ CAR TRAVEL

You may not be able to get by without a rental car in Provo, depending on where you're staying. Especially on your first trip, it's wise to plan on renting a car for at least a couple of days for some exploration, then you should decide whether you need it the rest of the week. Taxis can be expensive, with each round-trip equal in cost to a daily car rental, but if you feel uncomfortable driving on the left or if you want to go out and not worry about having too much to drink, then a taxi can be a good option. A car is the way to go if you want to do much exploring, because taxis will not wait for you in isolated areas. You will also need a car if you plan to snorkel at Smith's Reef, where you won't be able to call a taxi.

If you travel to North Caicos or Middle Caicos, you almost have to rent a car, because everything is so spread out. On the other islands, you can get by just walking or taking an occasional taxi.

To rent, you do need to have a valid U.S. license to drive, and you need to be 25 or older. **As of October 1, 2013, you also need a temporary local driving permit, which costs $30 (good for 1 to 90 days). You can pay the fee at the car-rental office.**

### GASOLINE

Gasoline is much more expensive than in the United States. Expect to pay about $2 to $3 more a gallon. There are numerous gas stations around Provo, but most accept only cash. The Texaco on Leeward Highway at the roundabout to Seven Stars is the only one that takes credit cards.

## PARKING

Parking in the Turks and Caicos is easy and free, and there are paved public accesses to all the beaches on Provo. Grace Bay has numerous public parking lots up and down its 12 miles (18 km). And all the resorts and restaurants offer free parking; even those that are gated have general public areas to park. North and Middle Caicos also have parking areas at all the restaurants and places to stay. You probably won't have a car on any of the other islands, but all the hotels have some free parking spots.

## RENTAL CARS

Avis and Budget have offices on the islands. You might also try local Provo agencies such as Grace Bay Car Rentals, Rent a Buggy, Tropical Auto Rentals, and Caicos Wheels—the latter rents scooters, colorful ATVs, cars, and even cell phones (some companies include a pay-as-you-go cell phone with a car rental).

On Provo, small cars start at around $39 per day, and a small high-clearance vehicle averages about $69 to $85 a day. All rental agencies in the Turks and Caicos will drop off a car for you at either the airport or your hotel. Upon return, you can always leave it at the airport. All the companies are fairly competitive and offer similar rates. All the companies offer cars with the steering wheel on the left (as in the United States) except for Grace Bay Car Rentals, which carries right-drive cars (as in the United Kingdom). Avis, Bayside, Budget, and Thrifty operate on Provo out of the airport; other local companies with off-airport locations include Caicos Wheels (which also rents dune buggies and scooters), Grace Bay Car Rentals, KK and T's Auto Rentals, Paradise Scooter and Auto (which also rents scooters and bicycles and runs Vespa tours), Rent a Buggy, Scooter Bob's (which also rents scooters).

Tony's Car Rental is the only car-rental company on Grand Turk. You can rent a car from Tony and explore on your own, or you can hire him to give you a guided tour. He will meet you at the airport and can also rent out snorkeling gear, scooters, jeeps, and Jet Skis. Alternatively, for $80 per day you can rent a golf cart from Nathan's Golf Cart Rental (you may be able to negotiate a lower rate if you're on the island for longer because much of Nathan's business is with cruise passengers). The island is small enough that it's more fun to get around by golf cart. The office is right outside the cruise ship port gates; on days no ship is in call before reaching Grand Turk. Nathan will meet you at the airport.

Al's Rent-a-Car and Pelican Car Rentals are on North Caicos.

**Contacts on Providenciales Avis** ✉ *Airport, Providenciales* ☎ *649/ 946–4705* ⊕ *www.avis.tc.* **Bayside Car Rentals.** $15 airport charge ✉ *Airport, Providenciales* ☎ *649/ 941–9010* ⊕ *baysidecarrentals.com.* **Budget** ✉ *Airport, Providenciales* ☎ *649/946–4079* ⊕ *www.budget.*

com. **Caicos Wheels** ⊠ *Grace Bay Ct., Grace Bay Rd., Grace Bay, Providenciales* ☎ *649/242–6592* ⊕ *www.CaicosWheels.com.* **Grace Bay Car Rentals** ⊠ *Grace Bay Plaza, Grace Bay Rd., Grace Bay, Providenciales* ☎ *649/941–8500* ⊕ *www.gracebaycarrentals.com.* **KK and T's Auto Rentals Ltd.** ⊠ *Long Bay Rd., Long Bay, Providenciales* ☎ *649/ 941–8377* ⊕ *www.kkntsautorentals. com.* **Paradise Scooter and Auto** ⊠ *Grace Bay Plaza, Grace Bay Rd., Grace Bay, Providenciales* ☎ *649/333–3333* ⊕ *www. paradisescooters.tc.* **Rent a Buggy** ⊠ *1081 Leeward Hwy., Leeward, Providenciales* ☎ *649/946–4158* ⊕ *www.rentabuggy.tc.* **Scooter Bob's** ⊠ *Turtle Cove, Providenciales* ☎ *649/ 946–4684* ⊕ *www.scooterbobstci. com.* **Thrifty** ☎ *649/946–4475* ⊕ *www.thriftytci.com.* **Tropical Auto Rentals** ⊠ *Tropicana Plaza, Leeward Hwy., The Bight, Providenciales* ☎ *649/946–5300* ⊕ *www. tropicalautorentaltci.-com.*

**Contacts on Grand Turk** **Nathan's Golf Cart Rental** ⊠ *Outside the gates, Grand Turk Cruise Terminal, Grand Turk* ☎ *649/946–1896.* **Tony's Car Rental** ⊠ *Grand Turk* ☎ *649/231–1806* ✉ *Thriller@tciway. tc* ⊕ *www.tonyscarrental.com.*

**Contacts on North Caicos** **Al's Rent-A-Car** ⊠ *Dock, North Caicos* ☎ *649/331–1947.* **Pelican Car Rentals** ⊠ *North Caicos* ☎ *649/241– 8275.*

## RENTAL CAR INSURANCE

Everyone who rents a car wonders whether the insurance that the rental companies offer is worth the expense. No one—including us—has a simple answer. If you own a car, your personal auto insurance may cover a rental to some degree, though not all policies protect you abroad; always read your policy's fine print. If you don't have auto insurance, then seriously consider buying the collision- or loss-damage waiver (CDW or LDW) from the car-rental company, which eliminates your liability for damage to the car. Some credit cards offer CDW coverage, but it's usually supplemental to your own insurance and rarely covers SUVs, minivans, luxury models, and the like. If your coverage is secondary, you may still be liable for loss-of-use costs from the car-rental company. But no credit-card insurance is valid unless you use that card for *all* transactions, from reserving to paying the final bill. All companies exclude car rental in some countries, so be sure to find out about the destination to which you are traveling. It's sometimes cheaper to buy insurance as part of your general travel insurance policy.

## ROADSIDE EMERGENCIES

If you find yourself stranded, chances are you'll be close to somewhere where you can ask for help, or someone sooner or later will go by that has a cell phone. Most rental companies have after-hours cell phones, and will either show up to help or bring you a new car. Keep emergency numbers (car-rental agency and your accommodation) with you, just in case. Picking up hitchhikers is not recommended.

## ROAD CONDITIONS

Most of Leeward Highway is a smooth, four-lane divided highway complete with roundabouts. However, the paved two-lane roads through the settlements on Providenciales can be quite rough, although signage is improving. A high-clearance vehicle is recommended if you want to head to Malcolm's Beach or if you're staying in the Turtle Tail area, those two areas have roads of rolled pack sand and have been known to have many potholes. The less-traveled roads in Grand Turk and the family islands are, in general, smooth and paved.

## RULES OF THE ROAD

Driving here is on the left side of the road, British style; when pulling out into traffic; remember to look to your right. Give way to anyone entering a roundabout, as roundabouts are still a relatively new concept in the Turks and Caicos; stop even if you are on what appears to be the primary road. And take them slowly; locals are quite used to seeing tourists and will keep their distance if they see you are struggling. The maximum speed is 40 mph (64 kph), 20 mph (30 kph) through settlements, and limits, as well as the use of seat belts, are enforced. Use extra caution at night, especially if you've had some drinks and don't remember to drive on the left. Although the police might not necessarily stop you, if you wreck you may have to be flown (expensively) to Miami. You will also be responsible for a new car. Don't be surprised if the car in front of you all of the sudden stops to say hello to someone, so always be on guard.

## ▌ TAXI TRAVEL

Taxis (actually large vans) on Providenciales are metered, and rates are regulated by the government. On the family islands (i.e., the smaller, outlying islands other than Provo), taxis may not be metered, so it's usually best to try to negotiate a cost for your trip in advance

On Provo, taxi rates are based on two people traveling together, but each additional person is charged extra; children should only pay half price—but always ask first. You may also be charged for more than two bags per person. Unless you have a rental car waiting for you at the airport, you will be taken to your resort by taxi. If you are using a taxi as your primary mode of transportation, get your driver's direct cell number. You will have to call for service, as they don't usually hang out anywhere except the airport. Taxi drivers are a great source of information about the islands, especially any political gossip, so if you find a good driver it's advisable to keep calling him directly. It's customary to tip about 10% per ride.

On other islands, taxis are usually available except on North Caicos, where you will need to rent a car if you want to get around, and Salt Cay, where they aren't necessary.

# ESSENTIALS

## ▌ ACCOMMODATIONS

Accommodations in the Turks and Caicos are not cheap, and though there's a wide range of price options, your accommodations will likely be your greatest expense. However, if you're prepared for this, you can find some unusual and memorable lodging experiences. There are many gorgeous villas in every size to choose from. Most of the resorts are made up of individually owned condos (not time-shares, but rather fully owned condominium units) placed in the hotel's rental pool when the owners are not in residence. Providenciales has two all-inclusive resorts: the family-oriented Beaches and the adults-only Club Med. There is only one time-share on the island, and it has a three-year waiting list for trade-ins. The outer islands have more basic and rustic accommodations.

If your accommodations don't include baby equipment or you need additional baby items, contact Happy Na and have it delivered. There's no need to lug everything you might need from home.

Contacts **Happy Na Baby Equipment Rentals**. If your accommodations don't provide everything you need, Happy Na can provide it for the day or (at a discount) for longer. The office is on Leeward Highway, and deliveries are made from 9 am to 8 pm daily. ☎ 649/941–5326 ✉ happyna@gmail.com.

### APARTMENT AND HOUSE RENTALS

Villa and condo rentals are quite common in the Turks and Caicos; in fact, they make up the majority of accommodations. On Provo most villas are ultraluxurious getaways, and have the prices to match. On the smaller islands, villas are basic and comfortable and tend to be more economical alternatives. Private apartment rentals can save you money but tend to be more residential, with fewer services. On any of the islands they are easy to book, and management companies will send a representative to meet you at the airport and lead the way.

Contacts **Home Away** ⊕ www.homeaway.com. **Turks and Caicos Reservations**. Based on the island, they keep inventory of villas and resorts, are in contact with general managers and property managements so, if in a bind, they can go the extra mile. ☎ 649/941–8988, 877/774–5486 ⊕ www.turksandcaicosreservations.tc. **Vacation Rentals by Owner** (*VRBO*). ⊕ www.VRBO.com.

### HOTELS

Hotels and resorts in Turks and Caicos run the gamut from small inns with basic accommodations to full-service, private-island resorts. There are a few classy boutique hotels on Provo, but no big chain hotels. Parrot Cay and the Meridian Club on Pine Cay are private-island resorts with all the pampering and privileges you'd expect for the high prices.

## █ COMMUNICATIONS

### INTERNET

The majority of resorts throughout the Turks and Caicos offer Wi-Fi service in their public areas, if not in the rooms, so you can keep up with email and the Internet.

### PHONES

The country code for the Turks and Caicos is 649. To call the Turks and Caicos from the United States, dial 1 plus the 10-digit number, which includes 649. Be aware that this is an international call. Calls from the islands are expensive, and many hotels add steep surcharges for long distance. Talk fast.

### CALLING WITHIN THE DESTINATION

To make local calls, just dial the seven-digit number. Most hotels and resorts charge for local calls, usually 50¢ a minute. Ask at the front desk if you need to dial "9" to get a dial tone; some require this for a line, in other places you just dial directly.

### CALLING OUTSIDE THE DESTINATION

To call the United States, dial 1, then the area code, and the seven-digit number. Remember that this is still an international call and will be charged accordingly. Since Hurricanes Irene and Sandy, international calls have not been going through properly. Depending on whether you are calling cell to landline, cell to cell, or land-

line to landline, you may have to try repeatedly to get through. You might get a recording stating the number is out of service.

---

### T&C LODGING TIPS

**Budget for the add-ons.** You must pay 12% tax, plus an additional 10% service charge.

**Avoid peak season.** Rates are about 35% higher from mid-December through mid-April.

**Book in advance.** Especially during peak season some resorts fill up quickly with repeat visitors.

**Reservations required.** You cannot enter the Turks and Caicos unless you have reserved a place to stay.

**Book direct.** You can sometimes get rates that are just as good (if not better) by booking directly through the resort, or using the local TurksandCaicosReservations.tc. For some condos you can book directly with the owner for less and avoid the service charge. (Ask about resort amenities; you might not get them all this way.)

**Know the terminology.** An "ocean view" may require you to stand on your tippy toes at a right angle. Some "garden view" rooms are just as nice for a better price.

**Consider your options.** Pampering is expensive; if you're low-maintenance, consider a self-catering apartment that will save you money on both food and resort services.

**Not sure where to stay?** Subscribe to *WhereWhenHow* magazine before you go, or click through the current issue online.

This is not usually the case. (The same thing can happen when you are calling a TCI number from another country.)

### CALLING CARDS

Calling cards are not recommended in Turks and Caicos, not even for international calls. They are hard to use, and you are charged even for toll-free connection numbers. It's actually cheaper to buy a simple "pay as you go" cell phone or a SIM card for your own unlocked mobile phone when you arrive.

### MOBILE PHONES

If you have a multiband phone (some countries use frequencies different from those used in the United States) and your service provider uses the world-standard GSM network (as do AT&T and T-Mobile—and to a lesser degree Verizon), you can probably use your phone abroad. Roaming fees can be steep, however—99¢ a minute is considered reasonable. And overseas you normally pay the toll charges for incoming calls. It's almost always cheaper to send a text message than to make a call, because text messages have a very low set fee (usually less than 50¢). You can usually buy an international package to get rates down. Service for Verizon can be unreliable here; AT&T service is good.

If your own cell phone doesn't work in the TCI, you can rent one from a local provider. All telephone service—both traditional and mobile—is provided by Lime and Digicel. Local cell-phone coverage is very good; you'll even get reception on the uninhabited cays. (Be

> ### CELL PHONE TIPS
>
> You can purchase a cheap cell phone at numerous outlets and simply "top-up" (pay as you go). Incoming calls are free, and with a local cell, you'll have service even on secluded and isolated beaches. Have your family call you to save on exorbitant island rates and high roaming charges.

aware, however, that Lime charges you for an international call when you dial a U.S. toll-free number from the Turks and Caicos.)

If you just want to make local calls, consider buying a new SIM card (note that your provider may have to unlock your phone for you to use a different SIM card) and a prepaid service plan in the destination. You'll then have a local number and can make local calls at local rates. If your trip is extensive, you could also simply buy a new cell phone in your destination, as the initial cost will be offset over time. Ask your car-rental company if they offer free loaner cell phones. Grace Bay Car Rentals is one that does; many other companies do as well these days. You can add value online or at kiosks all over the island, and incoming calls are free.

■TIP→ **If you travel internationally frequently, save one of your old mobile phones or buy a cheap one on the Internet; ask your cell phone company to unlock it for you, and take it with you as a travel phone, buying a new SIM card with pay-as-you-go service in each destination.**

**Contacts Digicel TCI** ⊕ *www. digiceltci.com.* **Lime** ☎ *649/946– 2200, 800/744–7777 for long distance, 649/266–6328 for Internet access, 811 for mobile service* ⊕ *www.time4lime.com.*

## ▌CUSTOMS AND DUTIES

Customs in the Turks and Caicos is straightforward and simple. On the flight you will receive two forms. The first is your customs declaration, and you should fill out one per family. The second form is a Turks & Caicos Embarkation and Disembarkation Form, which each person must fill out. Both forms must be filled out completely before you can get in the customs line. Make sure to keep the stub from the Disembarkation Form; you'll need to show it to leave the island. If you are 17 years old or older, you are allowed to bring in free of import duty 1 liter of spirits or 2 liters of wine; either 200 cigarettes *or* 100 cigarillos *or* 50 cigars *or* 250 grams of smoking tobacco, and 50 grams of perfume *or* 0.25 liters of eau de toilette. If you have $10,000 or more in cash you must declare it.

The immigration entrance lines can be long, especially when several planes arrive in quick succession. Make sure you have filled the forms completely before you get off the plane.

**Turks and Caicos Islands Information TCI Tourism** ⊕ *www.Turksand CaicosTourism.com.*

**U.S. Information U.S. Customs and Border Protection** ⊕ *www.cbp.gov.*

## ▌EATING OUT

The Turks and Caicos has almost any kind of restaurant you want, especially Provo. From small beach shacks to gorgeous upscale dining rooms and everything in between, this destination is a gastronomical delight. There are cafés and delis, international restaurants, and some of the best chefs in the Caribbean; what you won't find is fast food or restaurant chains. Typically, the restaurants offer wide choices, so even vegetarians and picky eaters will find something appealing on most menus. If a restaurant does not have a children's menu, the chef will usually be willing to make something to suit your kids, so don't be afraid to ask. Restaurants cater primarily to American tastes (especially on American holidays). Dinner usually starts a little later than Americans are used to; most restaurants are full by 8, and after dinner they are also the nightlife venues in this sleepy destination. Just bring a full wallet; most restaurants are upscale and expensive, though you will also find a few slightly less expensive, more casual options. A typical meal averages $80 to $120 per couple without a bottle of wine, even more if you add that in.

Unless otherwise noted, restaurants listed in this guide are open daily for lunch and dinner.

### TURKS AND CAICOS CUISINE

The most typical foods on these islands come from the sea. Grouper and snapper are usually the catch of the day, often grilled with jerk spices and sauces. Grouper is used in fish tacos at Hemingway's, giving a Caribbean twist to Mexican food. In season, spiny lobster is grabbed fresh from the ocean (the lobster Thermidor at Coyaba is insanely delicious). One favorite food in the Turks and Caicos is conch; so loved is this white meat from the sea that it even has its own festival in November, with recipe and tasting competitions. Conch is made every way imaginable, including in sushi. Macaroni and cheese or peas with rice are common side dishes, especially in spots that serve more local food. Coleslaw here even has a Caribbean twist, often including pineapple or mango. For a typical island breakfast, order broiled fish with baked beans and grits.

### PAYING

Most major credit cards (Visa, Discover, and MasterCard—Diner's Club less so) are accepted in restaurants. At this writing American Express is not accepted in the Turks and Caicos (except at IGA Gourmet supermarket). It's smart to bring more than one type of credit card with you just in case. Call your credit card company to see if they charge an additional foreign transaction fee; most do, even though all transactions in the TCI are in U.S. dollars. If a place takes cash only, it's noted on the review.

### RESERVATIONS AND DRESS

We only mention reservations when they are essential (there's no other way you'll ever get a table) or when they are not accepted. We mention dress only when men are required to wear a jacket or a jacket and tie. Although you don't

> ### WORD OF MOUTH
>
> Was the service stellar or not up to snuff? Did the food give you shivers of delight or leave you cold? Did the prices and portions make you happy or sad? Rate restaurants and write your own reviews in Travel Ratings or start a discussion about your favorite places in Travel Talk on www.fodors.com. Your comments might even appear in our books. Yes, you, too, can be a correspondent!

need fancy dresses or even long pants at most places, you will look out of place in T-shirts, jeans, and tennis shoes.

### WINES, BEER, AND SPIRITS

Major brands of liquor are widely available in the Turks and Caicos, but you may want to bring a bottle of your favorite with you, as there are no real duty-free bargains to be had. Imported U.S. beer is particularly expensive; a case of Bud Light or Miller Light can run $65 to $75. For beer lovers, it's always fun to try something new: the brewery for Turks Head, which is a heavier-tasting beer than its American counterparts, offers tours. Caicos rum is also made in the Turks and Caicos. A new Turks and Caicos Rum, called Bamberra Rum, has just been launched; it's a smooth blend of one of the best rums in the Caribbean, and a bargain compared to other rums. Some Caribbean brands are available in local stores, including Kalik and Red Stripe. Remember that although you can always buy alcohol at a bar, it's against the law to purchase it from a store on a Sunday.

## ▌ ELECTRICITY

Electricity is fairly stable through-out the islands, and the current is suitable for all U.S. appliances (120/240 volts, 60 Hz).

## ▌ EMERGENCIES

The emergency numbers in the Turks and Caicos are 999 or 911.

## ▌ HEALTH

Turks and Caicos is a safe and healthy destination. The tap water may not be the best tasting, but it is safe to drink. Food-safety stan-dards are high, and you rarely hear of upset stomachs or outbreaks of food poisoning. At this writing the Turks and Caicos do not have any major mosquito-borne ill-nesses like dengue fever, which has been a problem on many Carib-bean islands, but there are no-see-ums at dusk, and they really like to bite your ankles. Grace Bay Beach is usually clean and clear of any pests. Occasionally you'll run across a stray stingray; make sure not to step on its tail and you'll be fine. There are no poisonous snakes in the Turks and Caicos.

### OVER-THE-COUNTER REMEDIES

Most of the supplies are similar to those in the United Kingdom, United States, and Canada. You can find all the major brands that you are used to readily available around Provo, though prices are higher than at home. Over-the-counter drugs can be found at pharmacies and supermarkets, and even at small convenience stores. If you plan to travel beyond Provo,

however, you may wish to stock up on necessities. Supplies may be slimmer in the less-developed islands. Sunscreen is especially expensive in the Grace Bay area; it's more reasonably priced at the IGA supermarket. If you need bug spray, get something with at least 25% DEET; off-brand spray is readily available. If you forget to buy it and find yourself at dusk with no-see-ums biting, ask your servers at the restaurant; there's a good chance they'll have a bot-tle on hand.

**Health Warnings National Centers for Disease Control & Prevention** (*CDC*). ☏ 877/394–8747 *international travelers' health line* ⊕ *www.cdc.gov/travel.* **World Health Organization** (*WHO*). ⊕ *www.who.int.*

## ▌ HOURS OF OPERATION

Banks are typically open weekdays from 9 to 4. Post offices are open weekdays from 10 to 4. Shops are generally open weekdays from 10 to 5 or 6; most shops are closed on Sunday. You cannot buy alcohol anywhere in the islands on Sun-day except at a bar or restaurant.

### HOLIDAYS

Public holidays are New Year's Day, Commonwealth Day (sec-ond Monday in March), Good Friday, Easter Monday, National Heroes Day (last Monday in May), Queen's Birthday (third Monday in June), Emancipation Day (first Monday in August), National Youth Day (last Monday in Sep-tember), Columbus Day (second Monday in October), International Human Rights Day (last Monday in October), Christmas Day, and Boxing Day (December 26).

## ▌ MAIL

The post office is in downtown Provo at the corner of Airport Road (stamp collectors will be interested in the wide selection of stamps sold by the Philatelic Bureau, which maintains a small desk at the airport). You'll pay 50¢ to send a postcard to the United States, 60¢ to Canada and the United Kingdom; letters, per ½ ounce, cost 60¢ to the United States, 80¢ to Canada and the United Kingdom. When writing to the Turks and Caicos Islands, be sure to include the specific island and "Turks & Caicos Islands, BWI" (British West Indies). In general, the post office is not very reliable, and packages take an especially long time to arrive. There is no home delivery of mail; everyone has a PO Box. Expect postcards to take a month to get to your friends and neighbors—if they get them at all.

### SHIPPING PACKAGES

FedEx has offices on Provo and Grand Turk. Though expensive, FedEx is the only reliable way to send something to or from the islands. Keep in mind that buildings aren't numbered, though everyone on the island knows where each place is. Villas have names and not numbers, and there is no home delivery on any of the islands (even by FedEx); people must pick up packages at the FedEx office.

**FedEx** ☎ 649/946–4682 on Provo.
**Philatelic Bureau** ☎ 649/946–1534.

## ▌ MONEY

Prices quoted in this chapter are in U.S. dollars, which is the official currency in the islands.

Major credit cards and traveler's checks are accepted at many establishments. Bring small-denomination bills to the less populated islands—but bring enough cash to hold you over; many of the smaller islands deal in cash only and have no ATMs. Some islands don't even have banks, so get some cash while on Provo if heading elsewhere.

Prices throughout this guide are given for adults. Substantially reduced fees are almost always available for children, students, and senior citizens.

### ATMS AND BANKS

On Provo, there are ATMs at all bank branches (Scotiabank and First Caribbean), at the airport, Graceway IGA Supermarket, at Ports of Call shopping center, and at IGA Gourmet Supermarket. There are also Scotiabank and First Caribbean branches on Grand Turk.

### CREDIT CARDS

It's a good idea to inform your credit-card company before you travel, especially if you're going abroad and don't travel internationally very often. Otherwise, the credit-card company might put a hold on your card owing to unusual activity—not a good thing halfway through your trip.

Record all your credit-card numbers—as well as the phone numbers to call if your cards are lost or stolen—in a safe place, so you're prepared should something go wrong. All the major credit card companies have general numbers you can call (collect if you're abroad) if your card is lost, but you're better off calling the number of your issuing bank, because MasterCard and Visa usually just transfer you to your bank; your bank's number is usually printed on your card.

If you plan to use your credit card for cash advances, you'll need to apply for a PIN at least two weeks before your trip. Although it's usually cheaper (and safer) to use a credit card abroad for large purchases (so you can cancel payments or be reimbursed if there's a problem), note that some credit-card companies *and* the banks that issue them add substantial percentages to all foreign transactions, whether they're in a foreign currency or not. Check on these fees before leaving home, so there won't be any surprises when you get the bill.

Some shops require a $25 minimum to charge. A few shops may pass along their 3% to 5% surcharge if you pay by credit card; the clerk will tell you before you pay.

At this writing, American Express is currently not accepted for transactions except at the Graceway IGA on Providenciales.

**Reporting Lost Cards**

**American Express** ☎ 800/992–3404 in U.S., 336/393–1111 collect from abroad ⊕ www.americanexpress.com. **MasterCard** ☎ 800/627–8372 in U.S., 636/722–7111 collect from abroad ⊕ www.mastercard.com. **Visa** ☎ 800/847–2911 in U.S., 410/581–9994 collect from abroad ⊕ www.visa.com.

# ▌ PACKING

Most accommodations in Provo have washers and dryers in the units, so pack light. You can wash your clothes conveniently at your whim and dry swimsuits before repacking. If your resort doesn't offer laundry facilities or a laundry service, you'll find a dry cleaner next to Beaches and a Laundromat on Leeward Highway. Do not forget sunglasses; the sun is strong, and it's expensive to buy a new pair here. If you travel with a carry-on, airlines only allow 3-ounce bottles of liquids; don't worry, it's not too expensive to buy sunscreen at the Graceway IGA supermarket. There's really not a huge bug problem in the Turks and Caicos, but sometimes after rain or at dusk you might get a bite or two, so either buy or bring some Off.

For women, sundresses are fine for the nicest restaurant, and for men tropical-print shirts will do nicely. Almost all the resorts and villas have hair dryers and give you shampoo, conditioner, and a small box of laundry detergent. "Bring half the clothes and twice the money"—words to live by.

## PASSPORTS AND VISAS

U.S. citizens must have a valid passport to travel by air to the Turks and Caicos. Everyone must have an ongoing or return ticket and a confirmed hotel reservation. Make sure to keep the embarkation stub that you filled out when you landed, you'll need it when you leave.

## RESTROOMS

There are public restrooms and a playground in between Gansevoort and Aquamarine Beach Houses, for those times when you haven't realized how far you've walked.

## SAFETY

Although crime is not a major concern in the Turks and Caicos Islands, petty theft does occur here, and you're advised to leave your valuables in your hotel safe-deposit box and lock doors in cars and rooms when unattended. Small petty thefts have been known to happen, especially near construction sites (which are common, especially on Provo). Do all of the things your parents taught you: Don't walk in dark areas, especially the beach at night; don't leave valuables in a car unattended; if you wouldn't do it at home, don't do it here.

■TIP➔ **Distribute your cash, credit cards, IDs, and other valuables between a deep front pocket, an inside jacket or vest pocket, and a hidden money pouch. Don't reach for the money pouch once you're in public.**

## TAXES

The departure tax is $35 and is usually included in the cost of your airline ticket. If not, it's payable only in cash or traveler's check. Restaurants and hotels add a 10% government tax. Hotels also typically add 10% to 15% for service.

## TIME

The Turks and Caicos are in the Eastern Time Zone, the same as New York City and Atlanta. Unlike most Caribbean destinations, the Turks and Caicos do follow Daylight Savings Time when the United States does—except, oddly, at Club Med, which does not change its clocks, making them an hour earlier than those on the rest of the island during months when Daylight Savings Time is in effect.

## TIPPING

In restaurants, check your bill to see if a 10% service charge has been added; if yes, then supplement it by 5%, or even more if service was outstanding. If no service charge has been added, then tip as you would at home, about 15%. Taxi drivers also expect a tip, about 10% of your fare.

## TRIP INSURANCE

Comprehensive travel policies typically cover trip-cancellation and interruption, letting you cancel or cut your trip short because of a personal emergency, illness, or, in some cases, acts of terrorism in your destination. Such policies also cover evacuation and medical care. Some also cover you for trip delays because of bad weather or mechanical problems as well as for lost or delayed baggage. Another type of coverage to look for is financial default—that is, when your trip is disrupted because a tour operator, airline, or cruise line goes out of business. Generally you must buy this when you book your trip or shortly thereafter, and it's only available to you if your operator isn't on a list of excluded companies.

At the very least, consider buying medical-only coverage. Neither Medicare nor some private insurers cover medical expenses anywhere outside of the United States (including time aboard a cruise ship, even if it leaves from a U.S. port). Medical-only policies typically reimburse you for medical care (excluding that related to preexisting conditions) and hospitalization abroad, and provide for evacuation. You still have to pay the bills and await reimbursement from the insurer, though.

Another option is to sign up with a medical-evacuation assistance company. A membership in one of these companies gets you doctor referrals, emergency evacuation or repatriation, 24-hour hotlines for medical consultation, and other assistance. International SOS Assistance Emergency and AirMed International provide evacuation services and medical referrals. MedjetAssist offers medical evacuation.

Expect comprehensive travel insurance policies to cost about 4% to 7% or 8% of the total price of your trip (it's more like 8%–12% if you're over age 70). A medical-only policy may or may not be cheaper than a comprehensive policy. Always read the fine print of your policy to make sure that you are covered for the risks that are of most concern to you. Compare several policies to make sure you're getting the best price and range of coverage available.

■ TIP→ **OK. You know you can save a bundle on trips to warm-weather destinations by traveling during hurricane season. But there's also a chance that a severe storm will disrupt your plans. The solution? Look for hotels and resorts that offer storm/hurricane guarantees. Although they rarely allow refunds, most guarantees do let you rebook later if a storm strikes.**

**Insurance Comparison Sites**
**Insure My Trip.com** ☎ *800/487–4722* ⊕ *www.insuremytrip.com.*
**Square Mouth.com** ☎ *800/240–0369, 727/490–5803* ⊕ *www.squaremouth.com.*

**Medical Assistance Companies**
**AirMed International Medical Group** ⊕ *www.airmed.com.* **International SOS** ⊕ *www.internationalsos.com.* **MedjetAssist** ⊕ *www.medjetassist.com.*

**Medical-Only Insurers International Medical Group** ☎ *800/628–4664* ⊕ *www.imgglobal.com.* **Wallach & Company** ☎ *800/237–6615, 540/687–3166* ⊕ *www.wallach.com.*

Comprehensive Travel Insurers
**Allianz Global Assistance**
☎ *866/884-3556* ⊕ *www.*
*allianztravelinsurance.com.* **CSA**
**Travel Protection** ☎ *800/873-9855*
⊕ *www.csatravelprotection.com.*
**HTH Worldwide** ☎ *610/254-8700*
⊕ *www.hthworldwide.com.* **Travelex**
**Insurance** ☎ *888/228-9792* ⊕ *www.*
*travelex-insurance.com.* **Travel**
**Guard** ☎ *800/826-4919* ⊕ *www.*
*travelguard.com.* **Travel Insured**
**International** ☎ *800/243-3174*
⊕ *www.travelinsured.com.*

## ▌ VISITOR INFORMATION

The tourist offices on Grand Turk
and Providenciales are open daily
from 9 to 5.

Contacts **Turks & Caicos Islands**
**Tourist Board** ☎ *954/568-6588*
*in Ft. Lauderdale, 800/241-0824*
⊕ *www.turksandcaicostourism.com.*

ONLINE TRAVEL TOOLS
To make the most of your vacation, check out the website for
WhereWhenHow magazine,
which has links to everything
in the Turks and Caicos and an
extensive dining guide. A great up-
to-the-minute resource for events
and specials can be found at the
website for Enews; it's updated
every Wednesday. For everything
you need to know about Salt Cay,
there's a comprehensive website.

Contacts **Enews** ⊕ *www.TCIEnews.*
*com.* **Salt Cay** ⊕ *www.SaltCay.*
*org.* **WhereWhenHow** ⊕ *www.*
*WhereWhenHow.com.*

# INDEX

## A

Adventure tours, 126
Air travel, 16, 27, 144–146
Alcoholic drinks, 154
Alexandra Resort ☷ , 61
Alicia Shulman Jewelry, 85
Amanyara ☷ , 70
Ambergris Cay, 111
Anacaona✕ , 41–42
Anani Spa at Grace Bay Club, 81
Angela's Top o' the Cove New York Style Delicatessen✕ , 54
Anna's Art Gallery & Studio, 83
Apartment rentals, 150
Art and craft galleries, 83, 86
ArtProvo gallery, 83
Atlantic Bar & Grill✕ , 53
ATMs, 156
Atrium ☷ , 71

## B

Baci Ristorante✕ , 54–55
Bamberra Beach, 106
Banana boats, 24
Banks, 156
Barracuda Beach Bar ✕ , 100–101
Bars
Grand Turk, 130
Providenciales, 88
Bay Bistro✕ , 42
Beach dining, 42
Beach House Restaurant ✕ , 53
Beaches, 18
Caicos and the Cays, 103, 106–107, 110–111
Grand Turk, 119–120
Providenciales, 37–40
Salt Cay, 6
Beaches Red Line Spa, 81

Beaches Turks & Caicos Resort & Spa ☷ , 61
Bella Luna Ristorante✕ , 42
Belle Sound, 110
Belongers, 101
Bicycling
Grand Turk, 126–127
Providenciales, 71
Big Sand Cay, 136
Big Water Cay, 38
Bight, The, 32, 37, 53–54, 68–69, 85
Birdcage Restaurant✕ , 120
Bird-watching, 22, 86
Blue Hills, 36, 57–58
Blue Horizon Resort ☷ , 106
Blue Mountain, 35
Blue Water White Sands Resort ☷ , 62
Boat and ferry travel, 30, 146
Boating, 72–73
Bohio Dive Resort & Spa ☷ , 126
Boiling Hole, 109
Books for the beach, 98
Bookstores, 86
Bugaloo's ✕ , 58

## C

Cabana Bar & Grill✕ , 44
Caicos and the Cays, The, 14, 91–112
dining, 92–94, 100–103, 104, 106, 109–110
exploring, 94–95, 100, 104, 109
islands of, 94–112
lodging, 92–93, 96, 103, 106, 110
sports and the outdoors, 111–112
top reasons to go, 95
transportation, 92
Caicos Café✕ , 44

Caicos Conch Farm, 24, 32, 67
Caicos Dream Tours, 72
Caicos Wear Boutique, 83
Calling cards, 152
Capt. Hook's Grill ✕ , 123
Caribbean Paradise Inn ☷ , 62
Car rentals, 16, 147–148
Car travel, 16, 30, 146–149
roadside emergencies, 148
Casablanca Casino, 89
Casinos, 89
Castaway Salt Cay ☷ , 140
Cave tours, 107
Chalk Sound, 34, 39, 58
Chalk Sound National Park, 34
Charitable organizations, 74
Charter flights, 146
Cheshire Hall, 33
Children, attractions for, 24, 32, 34, 72, 86, 100, 104, 118
Climate, 21
Clothing shops, 83
Club Med Turkoise ☷ , 62
Cockburn Town, Grand Turk
dining, 120, 122
exploring, 117–119
lodging, 125
Coco Bistro✕ , 44–45
Como Shambhala at Parrot Cay, 82, 99
Conch, 67
Conch Bar Caves, 104
Conch Farm, 24, 32, 67
Concierge services, 61
Coral Gardens ☷ , 24, 68
Coral Reef Bar and Grill✕ , 137

Corner Café ✕ , 57
Coyaba Restaurant ✕ , 45
Crabtree Apartments ▥ , 125
Credit cards, 10, 156–157
Cruise activities, 128
Crystal Seas Adventures, 141
Cuisine of Turks and Caicos, 153–154
Currency, 16
Customs, 153

**D**

Da Conch Shack ✕ , 57
Daniel's Cafe ✕ , 104
Danny Buoy's Irish Pub ✕ , 45, 88
Deck at Seven Stars, 45–46
Dellis Cay, 97
Development, 23, 102
Dining, 153–154. ⇨ Also specific islands
beach dining, 42
cuisine of Turks and Caicos, 153–154
paying, 154
reservations and dress, 154
symbols related to, 10
tipping, 158
weekly specials, 44
wines, beer and spirits, 154
Discovery Bay, 33, 57, 86–87
Diving and snorkeling, 19–20
Caicos and the Cays, 111–112
Grand Turk, 127–128, 129
Providenciales, 73–76
Salt Cay, 141
West Caicos, 89
Dogs, 70
Dolphin Pub ✕ , 110
Duties, 153

**E**

East Caicos, 110
Electricity, 16, 155
Emergencies, 155
roadside emergencies, 148

**F**

Fauna, 22
Festivals and events, 21
Fishing, 18–19
Caicos and the Cays, 112
Providenciales, 76
Five Cays, 34, 58
Flamingo Cafe ✕ , 46
Flamingo Pond, 100
Flamingos, 86
Flora, 22
Food shops, 47, 83–85, 87
Fort George Cay, 96–97
FOTTAC (shop), 84
Fresh Bakery & Bistro ✕ , 56
Fresh Catch ✕ , 46
Full moon parties, 88

**G**

Gansevoort Turks & Caicos ▥ , 68
Gasoline, 146–147
Geography of Turks and Caicos, 22
Gibb's Cay, 24
Glowworms, 39
Goldsmith, The (shop), 129
Golf, 77
Gourmet Goods (shop), 84
Governor's Beach, 119
Grace Bay, Providenciales, 31, 37, 83–85
dining, 41–52
lodging, 61–68
Grace Bay Club ▥ , 62
Grace Bay Suites ▥ , 62
Grace's Cottage ✕ , 46
Graceway Gourmet (shop), 84
Graceway IGA Supermarket, 87

Grand Turk, 14, 113–130
beaches, 119–120
dining, 115, 117, 120–123
exploring, 117–119
lodging, 115, 125–126
nightlife, 130
shopping, 129
sports and the outdoors, 126–129
top reasons to go, 118
transportation, 115
Grand Turk Cruise Terminal, 120, 123, 126
Grand Turk Inn Bed & Breakfast ▥ , 125
Grand Turk Lighthouse, 119
Green flash, 26–27
Greenbean ✕ , 55
Greensleeves gallery, 86
Grill Rouge at Grace Bay Club ✕ , 47
Guanahani Restaurant & Bar ✕ , 122

**H**

Half Moon Bay, 38
Harbour Club Villas ▥ , 69
Health concerns, 155
Helicopter tours, 77
Hemingway's ✕ , 47–48
Her Majesty's Prison, 24, 117
Higg's Cafe ✕ , 101–102
History of Turks and Caicos, 12–13
Hole in the Wall ✕ , 56
Holidays, 155–156
Hollywood Beach Suites ▥ , 103
Home decor shops, 85
Horse Eye Jacks Beach Bar and Grill ✕ , 57
Horseback riding, 77
Horse Stable Beach, 103
Hours of operation, 155–156
House rentals, 139, 150
Hurricanes, 124

**I**

**Insurance**
*for car rentals, 148*
*trip insurance, 158–160*
**Inter Decor** (shop), 85
**Internet access,** 151
**Island Club Town-**
**houses** 🔟 , 64
**Island Pride** (shop), 87
**Island Thyme Bistro**✕ ,
138
**Island Vibes,** 72

**J**

**Jack's Shack** ✕ , 123
**Jai's** (shop), 85
**Jewelry shops,** 85, 87
**Jimmy Buffet's Margari-**
**taville**✕ , 123
**Jimmy's Dive Bar**✕ , 48

**K**

**Kew, North Caicos,** 100
**Kissing Fish Catering**
**Co.,** 84–85

**L**

**La Vista Azul** 🔟 , 69
**Las Brisas Restaurant &**
**Bar**✕ , 58
**Last Chance Bar and**
**Grill** ✕ , 102
**Le Bouchon de Village**
✕ , 48
**Le Vele** 🔟 , 64
**Leeward,** 32, 38, 56, 71
**Lighthouses,** 119
**Liquor shops,** 86
**Little Ambergris Cay,**
111
**Little Water Cay,** 24, 94
**Lodging,** 17. ⇨ Also specific islands
*accommodation options,*
*60, 150–151*
*coming attractions, 23,*
*102*
*concierge services, 61*
*money-saving tips, 151*
*symbols related to, 10*
*tipping, 158*
*villa rentals, 60*

**Long Bay** (Providencia-
les), 38
**Long Bay** (South Caicos),
111
**Lower Bight Beach,** 37
**LunaSea Pool Bar abd**
**Grill** ✕ , 48

**M**

**Magnolia Wine Bar &**
**Restaurant**✕ , 55
**Mail,** 156
**Making Waves Art Stu-**
**dio,** 83
**Malcolm's Beach,** 40
**Mama's** (shop), 85
**Mango Reef** ✕ , 49
**Meridian Club** 🔟 , 96
**Middle Caicos,** 24, 104,
106–107, 108
**Middle Caicos Cafe**
✕ , 53
**Miss Moonies** ✕ , 49
**Miss Moonies** 🔟 , 64
**Mobile phones,** 152–153
**Money matters,** 16, 17,
36, 156–157
**Mookie Pookie Pizza**
**Palace**✕ , 120, 122
**Mudjin Bar and Grill**
✕ , 106
**Mudjin Harbour,** 24, 106
**Museums,** 24, 118–119

**N**

**North Ridge,** 119
**North Beach,** 136
**North Caicos,** 99–103,
105
**Northwest Point,** 37, 40,
58–59, 70
**Northwest Point**
**Resort** 🔟 , 70

**O**

**Ocean Club** 🔟 , 64
**Ocean Club West** 🔟 ,
64–65
**Ocean Escapes Spa,** 129
**Online travel tools,** 160
**Opus**✕ , 49

**Osprey Beach Hotel** 🔟 ,
125, 130
**Over-the-counter drugs,**
155

**P**

**Packing,** 157
**Paddleboarding,** 78
**Parallel 23**✕ , 49–50
**Parasailing,** 78
**Parking,** 147
**Parrot Cay,** 97–99
**Parrot Cay Resort** 🔟 , 98
**Passports,** 16, 158
**Pat's Place**✕ , 137
**Pelican Bay** ✕ , 50
**Pelican Beach,** 38
**Pelican Beach Hotel** 🔟 ,
103
**Phones,** 16, 151–153
**Photography,** 99
**Pillory Beach,** 120, 122,
126
**Pine Cay,** 95–96
**Piranha Joe's** (shop),
129
**Pirate's Hideaway &**
**Blackbeard's Quar-**
**ters** 🔟 , 140
**Pizza Pizza**✕ , 50
**Playground,** 24
**Plunge at Regent**
**Palms**✕ , 50
**Point Grace** 🔟 , 65
**Porter's Island Thyme**
**Bistro** ✕ , 138
**Ports of Call Resort**
🔟 , 65
**Potcakes,** 70
**Price categories,** 10, 41
**Prisons,** 24, 117
**Private Chef Turks and**
**Caicos,** 85
**Private villas,** 60
**Providenciales,** 14,
25–89
**Provo Golf & Country**
**Club,** 77

**Q**

**Quality Supermarket,** 87

**R**

Rake-and-scrape music, 130

Reef Residences ⬚, 68–69

Regent Grand Resort ⬚, 65

Regent Palms ⬚, 65

Regent Spa, 82

Restaurant at Amanyara, 58–59

Restrooms, 158

Road conditions, 149

Ron Jon Surf Shop, 129

Royal Jewels (shop), 87

Royal West Indies Resort ⬚, 66

Rules of the road, 149

**S**

Safety, 158

Sailing, 72–73

Salt Cay, 14, 131–142

Salt Cay Salt Works, 142

Salt Raker Inn ⬚, 125, 130

Sand Bar ✕, 122

Sands at Grace Bay ⬚, 66

Sandy Point Beach, 103

Santa Maria Gambling Saloon, 130

Sapodilla Bay, 39

Sapodilla Hill, 34

Seaside Café ✕, 50

Secret Garden ✕, 122

Seven ✕, 51

Seven Stars ⬚, 66

Sharkbites Bar & Grill ✕, 55–56

Shipping packages, 156

Shop at Grand Turk Inn, 129

Shopping
Grand Turk, 129
hours of operation, 155–156
Providenciales, 47, 80–87
Salt Cay, 142

Sibonné Beach Hotel ⬚, 66

Silver Deep Boutique, 85

Silver Palms Restaurant ✕, 102–103

Smokey's on Da Bay ✕, 51

Snorkeling. ⇨ See Diving and snorkeling

Somerset, The ⬚, 66–67

Somewhere on the Beach Café and Lounge ✕, 54

South Caicos, 107, 109–112

South Caicos Ocean & Beach Resort ⬚, 110

Souvenir shops, 81, 85, 87

Spas, 80–83, 99

Spa Sanay, 82

Spa Tropique, 82

Stelle ✕, 54

Supermarkets, 47, 87

Symbols, 10

**T**

Taxes, 158

Taxis, 16, 27, 35, 149

tipping, 158

Taylor Bay, 39

Tennis, 78

Teona Spa, 82

Thalasso Spa at Point Grace, 83

Three Mary Cays, 100

Three Mary Queens ✕, 57–58

Tiki Hut ✕, 56

Time, 158

Tipping, 158

Tour options, 78–79

Tradewinds Guest Suites ⬚, 140

Transportation, 144–149

Trip insurance, 158–160

Turks & Caicos National Museum, 24, 118–119

Turks & Caicos National Trust (shop), 87

Turtle Cove, Providenciales, 32, 86
dining, 54–56
lodging, 69–70

Turtle Cove Inn ⬚, 70

Turtle Tail, 32, 69

Tuscany, The ⬚, 67

**U**

Unicorn Bookstore, 86

Upstairs Bar & Grill ✕, 51

**V**

Venetian on Grace Bay ⬚, 67

Venetian Road, 32

Villa Del Mar ⬚, 68

Villa Renaissance ⬚, 68

Villa rentals, 60, 139

Villas of Salt Cay ⬚, 140

Visas, 158

Visitor information, 17, 160

Vix Bar and Grill ✕, 51–52

**W**

Wades Green, 100

Waterskiing, 79

Weather information, 21, 122, 124

Weddings, 17

West Bay Club ⬚, 69

West Caicos, 89

West Harbour, 35

West Harbour Bay, 40

Whale-watching, 141

When to go, 21

Whitby Beach, 103

White House, 136

White Sands Beach, 120

White Sands Beach Resort ⬚, 126

Wild Cow Run, 107

Windsong Resort ⬚, 69

Windsurfing, 79–80

Wine Cellar (shop), 86

**Y**

Yoshi's Japanese Restaurant ✕, 52

## Photo Credits

Front cover: SIME/eStock Photo [Description: Grace Bay Beach, Providenciales]. Spine: Vilainecrevette/Shutterstock. 1, Stephen Frink Collection / Alamy. 2, Jsnover I Dreamstime.com. 3 (top), Tropical Imaging. 3 (bottom), Big Blue Unlimited. 4 (top left), Ramunas Bruzas I Dreamstime.com. 4 (top right), Quinton Dean. 4 (bottom), Stephen Frink Collection / Alamy. 5 (top), Amanresorts. 5 (bottom), Aleksei Potov/ Shutterstock. 6 (top and bottom), Ramona Settle. 7, Stephen Frink Collection / Alamy. 8 (top left), idreamphoto / Shutterstock. 8 (top right), Ersler Dmitry / Shutterstock. 8 (bottom), Courtesy of Seven Stars Resort. Chapter 1: Experience the Turks and Caicos: 11, Terrance Klassen / age footstock. Chapter 2: Providenciales: 25, BlueOrange Studio / Shutterstock. Chapter 3: The Caicos and the Cays: 91, Abbie Enock / age fotostock. Chapter 4: Grand Turk: 113, Terrance Klassen / age fotostock. Chapter 5: Salt Cay: 131, Purestock/ age fotostock.

# NOTES

# Fodor's InFocus TURKS & CAICOS ISLANDS

**Publisher:** Amanda D'Acierno, *Senior Vice President*

**Editorial:** Arabella Bowen, *Executive Editorial Director*; Linda Cabasin, *Editorial Director*

**Design:** Fabrizio La Rocca, *Vice President, Creative Director*; Tina Malaney, *Associate Art Director*; Chie Ushio, *Senior Designer*; Ann McBride, *Production Designer*

**Photography:** Melanie Marin, *Associate Director of Photography*; Jessica Parkhill and Jennifer Romains, *Researchers*

**Maps:** Rebecca Baer, *Senior Map Editor*; David Lindroth; *Cartographer*

**Production:** Linda Schmidt, *Managing Editor*; Evangelos Vasilakis, *Associate Managing Editor*; Angela L. McLean, *Senior Production Manager*

**Sales:** Jacqueline Lebow, *Sales Director*

**Marketing & Publicity:** Heather Dalton, *Marketing Director*; Katherine Fleming, *Senior Publicist*

**Business & Operations:** Susan Livingston, *Vice-President, Strategic Business Planning*; Sue Daulton, *Vice-President, Operations*

**Fodors.com:** Megan Bell, *Executive Director, Revenue & Business Development*; Yasmin Marinaro, *Senior Director, Marketing & Partnerships*

---

**Writer:** Ramona Settle

**Editor:** Douglas Stallings

**Production Editor:** Carolyn Roth

---

2nd Edition

ISBN 978-0-7704-3260-7

ISSN 1946–3049

## SPECIAL SALES

# ABOUT OUR WRITER

On a quest for the perfect beach, Ramona Settle chose the Turks and Caicos Islands for her future retirement home. When she's not visiting her home there with her family, she is working at her family's ice-cream stand in Virginia or taking pictures. Her photographs have been featured in the local publications *Times of the Islands* and *Where When How* magazines. She also answers questions for travelers in the Fodors. com travel forums. Obsessed with travel, she visits the Turks and Caicos as often as she can.